The
Magic World
Professor Hilton Hotema

ISBN: 978-1-63923-471-4

Printed: August 2022

Cover Art By: Paul Amid

Published and Distributed By:
Lushena Books
607 Country Club Drive, Unit E
Bensenville, IL 60106
www.lushenabks.com

ISBN: 978-1-63923-471-4

The Magic World
Professor Hilton Hotema

Table of Contents

Our Poisoned Earth & Sky

"And God saw that the wickedness of man was great in the earth, and that every imagination of the thoughts of his heart was only evil continually. And it repented God that He had made man on the Earth, and it grieved Him at His heart. And God said, I will destroy man whom I have created from the face of the earth. (Gen. 6:5-7)."

To All Whom It May Concern:

BE IT KNOWN ALL MEN BY THESE PRESENTS that statements in this volume are based on facts observed and facts inferred, the known and recognized laws of Creation, certain statements in the Bible, and other ancient scriptures and records, including stone monuments, as they have been discovered and interpreted.

No claim of any kind is made intentionally as to what any method cited may do for any one in any case, and each one acts on his own responsibility. It is recognized and understood that the author and the publisher of this work assume no obligation or responsibility for any opinion, presented or expressed, nor the results that may occur in any case wherein any one may decide- to pursue any path mentioned or inferred in this work.

The author of this work is not available for engagements of any kind, receives no visitors, grants no interviews, and has no desire to become Exhibit A for curiosity seekers. He has no message for any one other than those presented and contained in his writings, and he discusses with no one the subjects and matters about which he writes.

Professor Hilton Hotema
Honolulu, Hawaii, 1967

Special Notice By Publisher

This work is prepared and published for the benefit and enlightenment of mankind, permission is hereby granted to quote from it, provided full credit is given to author and publisher.

Freedom of Speech & of the Press

We believe in the inalienable and constitutional right of religious liberty, and freedom of speech and of the press as a means of education and conveying God's message to our fellow man, as is guaranteed by the first amendment to the Constitution, which reads:

"Congress shall make no law respecting an established religion, or prohibiting the free exercise thereof; or abridging the freedom of speech or the press; or the right of the people peaceably to assemble, and to petition the government for a redress of grievances."

The five Supreme Court Justices of the State of Florida appeared to be in harmony with this amendment when they showed in a case before them "what is really involved in any attempt to throttle free speech or to choke the press." Concurring in the decision with the others, Judge Chapman rendered a separate opinion, in which he said in part:

"The liberty and freedom of the press under our fundamental law is not confined to newspapers and periodicals, but embraces pamphlets, leaflets, and comprehends every publication which affords a vehicle of information and opinion. The perpetuity of

Democracies has as a foundation an informed, educated and intelligent citizenry. An unsubsidized press is essential to and a potent factor in instructive information and education of the people of a democracy and a well-informed people will perpetuate our constitutional liberties."

(Quoted In "Liberty," Vol. 37, No. 1, First Quarter 1942, P. 31.)

Testimonials of Readers of Hotema's Folios

The Hotema Folios are great. I can't stop reading them. Please send #1 and #2 Folios by Hotema on Live Longer — H. H. of N. Y.

Son of Perfection by Hotema is the best and most complete analysis I ever read of the secret of earth life and the method of individual redemption and "salvation." This reveals not only the "True Path to Atonement" but gives the lie to the frauds of all false teachings on this most important of all subjects —the Human Soul and its path to perfection. — P. G., California.

Rush another set of the Hotema folios. I'm lending the set I purchased to a friend, who says they are great. W. C. L., N. C.

I have difficulty laying down the Hotema folios long enough to write you to say I received them. It is thrilling to read works of an intellectually advanced person and find line after line explaining the things as I have pieced them out in my own serious studies and meditations. -- A. E. B., Kansas

Hotema's folios are really great. Please send Live Longer I and II by Hotema to my mother. — C. P., Alaska.

Hotema's folios astound me with the information they reveal. T. P., McG., N.Y.

I have just finished reading the Mysterious Sphinx. It is a jewel — it is light — More Light and Further Light — E. D. B., Washington.

We consider Prof. Hotema one of the world's greatest teachers. – Grant E. Hockens, N.Y.

After reading Hotema's writings for five years, I can see in him a many-incarnated being. He is on a much higher level of understanding, and lives in a world unknown to the multitude. This is clearly indicated by his thoughts in his writings, and shows that he has made the Cosmic Cycle of Creation many times to gain the great knowledge he expresses, much of which

goes over the head of the average individual. — H. G.,
Michigan.

Hotema's work on the Tarot presents many startling ideas I
never read before in any writings. He reveals the answers to
many puzzling and profound anthropological, biological and
psychological problems that have perplexed the best scholars for
ages.

It was left for Hotema to correlate and analyze all existing
data, as well as to decode the symbols and allegories of the
Ancient Masters, and to explain the facts and conclusions which
are of such immense value to mankind. — W. M. C. Lloyd,
North Carolina.

I was astonished when I read Hotema's folio 'How I Lived To
Be 90" to learn that he was a veteran of the Spanish-American
War, having been one of the soldiers who shot their way thru the
insurrection in the Philippines nearly 70 years ago. And of the
1325 men in his army regiment, he is now the only one living —
M. F. C., New York.

I have read the Magic Wand (Caduceus) and learned more
from it that my many years in one of the "Mystery" schools. How
wonderful it would be if only more people would find the Light
and Seek the Truth. — Dr. A. M. J., Illinois.

As a Spiritualistic Minister and Teacher, I have found that
because of human ignorance and fear, only a few are strong
enough to face the facts as Hotema has presented them. Having
to unlearn what one has been taught that is false requires far
greater effort than if one could start with a clean, blank sheet
and place thereon the facts of Life. — G. D. C., California.

Hotema is a thinker far above the best scientists, for he is not
afraid to oppose them and show where they are wrong. — A. F.,
California.

Hotema's Flame Divine surpasses everything I have ever read before and I'm studying it with unlimited enthusiasm. — Mrs. H. R. F., Florida.

The Great Red Dragon is to me an answer to my unconscious prayer for Light in the darkness. — W. B. H., Iowa.

We think the Mystery of Man is the most wonderful writing we have ever read. — W. T., California.

A reader fan of mine sent me your book 'Mystery Man of the Bible.' For over 40 years my beliefs have been along the lines of your book, which I regard as the greatest literary masterpiece of all time. Anyone who has read or studied the bible is certainly missing the most important part of his education if he does not read this book, and I recommend it most highly to my friends and enemies alike. Every man, woman and child should read it. — A. D. Barber, Managing Trustee, Barber Scientific Foundation, Washington, D.C.

Chapter No. 1 – Magic Intelligence

"An atom consists of a spheroidal form containing within itself a nucleus of life. Absolute intelligence appears in every atom" (Alice Bailey, in *A Treatise on Cosmic Fire,* p. 245). All created formations consist of billions of atoms, and, so far as we know, Cosmic Consciousness rules their basic activity.

This fact was recognized by Thomas A. Edison, greatest inventor America ever produced. He said: *"Consider the thousands of ways in which atoms of hydrogen combine with other atoms, forming the most diverse substances. Do you mean to say that atoms do this marvelous work without intelligent guidance?"*

Cells build bodies that are composed of atoms. And the innate knowledge of the part every cell must perform in the construction and sustentation of the body, whether tree or man, is a mode of action of the atom of every organized form, whether in tree or in man. They perform their magical work automatically and perfectly, as if they understood mathematics, chemistry, biology and physiology. And here we encounter another phase of fraud in this world of fraud. Just as in religion, so in the field of medicine, the masses must be deceived, duped, and kept in darkness.

The body's functions can never be out of order. The alleged disorders of a sick person are the symptoms of the body's struggle to save itself from the damage it has suffered, due to man's evil habits and adverse environment. It is not only wrong but actually dangerous for doctors to interfere with the body's saving struggle at such times, as they are taught to do by administering poison falsely called medicine. The body will save itself if permitted to do so; and the patient will recover if nothing is done to hamper the body's saving effort.

We speak from years of practical experience. We never lost a patient in our sanitarium, and most of them came to us after being given up to die by other doctors.

As additional evidence that we know our position is on solid ground, we presented in our work titled "*How I Lived to Be 90*" a chapter on The Dying Woman, a story that showed how easily and quickly we saved a woman's life after the best medic in the county had given her up to die.

In regard to these important matters, Rev. Win. L. Blessing, Pastor of House Of Prayer Church, in his remarkable publication titled "*Showers Of Blessing*" for April, 1967, made this statement:

"A billion tons of deadly poison are sprayed on crops every year in the United States. Almost all fruits and vegetables that you eat are loaded with these poisons. I predict that within fifty years from now the human race will be sterile or that one out of every two born will be a monster.

"We are simply letting billion-dollar chemical and pharmaceutical companies destroy us. The seventh and last plague is in the air. Medical doctors don't have a cure for any disease. They just prescribe the latest drugs, such as sulfur, auromycin and penicillin for everything. Fifty years ago it was pull the teeth, later it was remove the appendix. Now it's penicillin. They don't even have a cure for the common cold and no-thing that will touch influenza."

Prof. Lawrence Calton, in the "Family Circle" publication, took a telling shot at the same target. He said:

"*We are in the day of the pill. Tired? Have a pill to pep you up. Anxious? Have a pill to calm you down. Blue? Goble a pill to lift up your spirits. Feverish? Sleepless? Have a pill. Thanks to (the so-called progress of medical science and) the fervent belief* *that is growing for a pill for virtually everything, we're gulping medicine today at a fantastic rate. From $867,000,000 in 1947, manufacturers' sales of pharmaceuticals shot up to $1,600,000,000 in 1954, then up to $2,200,000,000 in 1957 — and are still climbing.*

"Total output of medicinals in the United States now exceeds 101,400,000 pounds. Thirteen hundred tons of antibiotics and 4,900 tons of vitamins are being turned out annually. Sales of hormones — extremely potent drugs taken in tiny doses — have reached 46,000 pounds. More than 50,000,000 prescriptions for tranquilizers, not to mention other mood-changing drugs, were written last year."

The Bible referred to this matter three thousand years ago, and said: *"Thou hest no healing medicines. ... In vain shalt thou use many medicines."* — Jer. 30:13; 46:11). There would be no religion if the hidden facts of life were known. There would be no medical profession if the hidden facts of sickness were known.

Sickness cost the deluded people in this country forty billion dollars in 1964, according to press reports. A business that drags in the dollars at that rapid rate must be protected by every hook and crook that can be used. The magic, conscious, objective mind of man appears as Intelligence rising from the activity of the atoms in his body, and manifesting in his brain as the result of nervous action and sensation.

All phases of consciousness, from the lowest to the highest, should appear in man. For he is the Supreme Being of all created formations known. And such was the case in the early days, before man sank so low in the realm of life, due to evil habits and adverse environment. Because man can think, he stands as ruler of this globe and of the animals that inhabit it with him. "Know thyself" was written above the entrance to the great Greek temples. Cervantes, the Spaniard, advised: *"Make it thy business to know thyself, which is the most difficult lesson in the world."*

Napoleon, who used men as pawns and puppets, knew them better than any poet. He said, "Men in general are but children." John Sterling called man "A form clad in shadows."

The Psalmist said: "What is man, that Thou art mindful of him? Thou has made him a little lower than the angels, and hest crowned him with glory and honor. Thou madest him to have dominion over the works of Thy hands; Thou hast put all things under his feet" (Ps. 8:4-6).

Man is the key to the ancient scriptures and an integral part of that reality which represents universality.

Man is the Microcosm of the Macrocosm. He is the constellation of the powers that form the celestial bodies, the sun, moon, planets, and stars.

All powers of the universe are potentially contained in man. His body and organs are products and representatives of cosmic phenomena. No doctor should attempt to change, alter or interfere with the body's functions at any time, and especially during sickness. The body is always guided by Eternal Knowledge. Its functions are always controlled and directed by Cosmic Consciousness, and the purpose is always to preserve the body. The body knows its work, and knows always what to do, and how to do it, and will do it if given a chance.

1. Man is an infinitely compounded being, a living mirror of the universe; an embodiment of its powers and principles.

2. In man are summarized, recapitalized and perfectionized, all powers and principles of the universe.

3. As the highest known organization in the universe, man is the Supreme Being of the various kingdoms, as stated in the Bible (Gen. 1:26).

4. Man is the individualization of the universe, partaking of all its qualities and potentialities as the dew-drop partakes of all the qualities and potentialities of the ocean.

5. Man is supremely specialized Being of Creation, and his work is the most perfect specialization of the most complex individualization of the Abstract Principles of the Universe.

The first step in the study of Man is to free the mind of all the ologies and isms, all false theories of medicine, and all stupid dogmas of religion. We must notice again the work of the great scientist, Dr. Alexis Carrel. He died in 1944 at the age of 71 after he had amazed the medical world in his demonstration of the immortality of the cells of the body. Carrel kept the cells of a chicken's heart alive for 27 years after the death of the chicken (p. 173). The immortality of the cells indicates that man should live forever. And science agrees that such is possible. Famous in medical circles for his amazing discoveries, Carrel was a staff member of the Rockefeller Medical Research from 1906 to 1939. In 1912 he won the Nobel Prize.

This noted scientist was so profoundly impressed by the paucity of knowledge possessed by medical science as to Man, and the scanty information he was able to gather in his life-work on the subject of Man, that he was inspired to write his wonderful book of 364 pages, published in 1935, titled *"Man the Unknown."*

At that time, we published a monthly magazine, titled How To Live For Health & Strength, and the publisher of the above book sent us a review copy. We were so deeply impressed with the knowledge contained in the book, that we ordered 100 copies at wholesale rate to sell to the readers of our magazine.

It was called a great book; but the leading feature of its greatness was the remarkable frankness of Carrel in publicly informing the world what all medics privately admit — that the practice of medicine is in darkness as dense now as to man and his ailments, as were the founding fathers of medicine a thousand years ago. By frequent repetition in his book, Carrel impressed the fact upon the world that "the science of man is still too rudimentary to be useful" (p. 179).

That statement by this great scientist plainly informs the world that medical science knows little about man, about the functions of his body, and less about the body's disorders. In plainer words, the medics are, by their own admission, nothing more than experimenters, and have never been anything else. And that is called Medical Science. But beware; do not be misled — for there is method in this madness. The medics don't want the world to know it. For the protection of medicine, everything that can be done is being done to keep the world in darkness as to human ailments, just as religion does everything that can be done to keep the masses in darkness as to the nature of Life and the constitution of man.

For the greedy purpose of exploitation by the sordid institutions that control civilization, the masses must be kept in darkness and ignorance to make them peaceful prey for their plunderers.

He who is so bold and unethical as to interfere with and obstruct this regular course by striving to enlighten the masses in this world of fraud, quickly becomes the target of the exploiters and plunderers. If his death is expedient to remove him from the path, so be it.

And so, Dr. Carrel was treading on treacherous ground when he published his wonderful book, so seriously needed by the world. It was such a hot number and so eagerly read, that the hard-cover edition went into 55 printings and was translated into 18 foreign languages. That shocked medical science and the drug industry. Some drastic action had to be taken. And so, Carrel was soon eased out of the Rockefeller Institute as the first step. Then he decided to return to France, his native land. Perhaps he had in mind the founding of a school there to teach the salient facts set forth in his book. That would never do.

It appears the authorities in France had been notified and were waiting for him. And they had their orders what to do with him when he arrived. When he reached France he was arrested (August 31, 1944) on a fraudulent charge, and cast into prison. After that his life was short. On November 5, 1944, he died suddenly of a reported "heart attack." Carrel was not the first, nor will he be the last who will perish because of his good efforts to enlighten the world.

Perhaps the greatest story presented in the Four Gospels is what happened to Jesus for his good work to enlighten the multitude. Read it again; we vote:

"Then gathered the chief priests and the Pharisees a council, and said, What do we? For this man doeth many miracles. If we let him thus alone, all men will believe on him; and the Romans will come and take away both our place and our nation.

"And one of them, named Caiaphas, being the high priest that same year, said unto them, YE KNOW NOTHING AT ALL, nor consider that it is expedient for us, that ONE MAN SHOULD DIE FOR THE PEOPLE, and that a whole nation perish not." (John 11:47-50).

That desperate work of the leaders is always done FOR THE PEOPLE. And the dumb, deceived, gullible masses believe it.

Chapter No. 2 – Magic World

"Every one during the days of Columbus actually believed the Earth was flat, as taught by the religionists. Yet even the Greeks of classic Antiquity knew it is a sphere, floating in space, moving in an easterly direction around the sun" (Astrology, by Joseph Goodavage, 1966).

With the fading of the Dark Ages, a Magic World is coming out of the shadows and a new science is being born. World events indicate we are entering the Space Age, and the clear light of objective reasoning is being experienced. This is forcing science to discard many of its outmoded methods to meet the surprising adventure of totally unexpected knowledge.

There is no longer any doubt that extraterrestrial forces have a powerful effect on all areas of existence — individual and collective. Every plant, beast, fish, fowl and insect respond to exogenous influences, which, for the most part, are forces unseen and unknown. Man is influenced by many cosmic forces. And it has always been known that animals respond to external stimuli called "instinct."

But what exactly is instinct? A terminology that fails to expound is useless. And is man, by virtue of his complexity, immune to instinct? Considering his highly-developed brain and nervous system, it would seem that man should be even more likely to react to exogenous forces than the less sensitive creatures.

Modern man credits himself with more knowledge and wisdom than all the ages of his ancestors. The evidence shows that he is wrong. And his science cannot explain the remnants of vast, highly-developed extinct civilizations, some of which are so old as to be dismissed as legends and myths, and they left behind huge structures, the crumbling terrains of which strike us with awe and wonder.

Contrary to the hypothesis of the evolutionist, man knows his species has existed in its present form for at least two million years. And he is too completely mind-conditioned to see any mystery in the fact that his recorded history is only a few thousand years old. And the brain-washing to which he is subjected causes him to subscribe to the theory of evolution. But no new species have ever appeared during man's entire history. His science and technology are the diamond-hard drills with which he plans to probe all the mysteries of physical nature. But he is surrounded by an ocean of evidence signifying a Non-Material Cause. The Ancient Magi knew much about the old world that is really new to us. Among other things, they invented a clever design, called the Zodiac, to describe in various ways the manner in which things in the Magic World are influenced by the celestial bodies of the Empyrean.

The solar system appears as a unit in this universe of galaxies, and the Ancient Magi discovered that man reacts and interacts with his terrestrial and celestial environment. That data is the basis of the Zodiac.

A few centuries ago, before astrology and astronomy diverged, a group of scientists tried to learn something about the interaction of the cosmos. They were astrologers.

History shows that astrology has influenced men in all ages. It is the historical record that is the foremost intellectual movement of all time. It predates all other sciences, all religions, and all political systems. It is older than the Egyptian Pyramids, the tablets of ancient Babylon, or the Ark of the Covenant.

Astrology fascinated Stoics in togas and Mystics in robes — the Popes of the Middle Ages and contemplative Buddhists — the prophets and priests who wrote the Bible.

Hippocrates taught that there is a cosmic correspondence for every rhythm, periodically, or cycle of time, whether applied to the Earth or to the life upon it. The Egyptians, Babylonians, Chaldeans, Sumerians and Phoenicians knew it. The Chaldeans and Sumerians deducted a cycle in the affairs of men and nations called Saros, which consisted of 3600 years. They had observed many Saros cycles.

Cicero stated that the Chaldeans had records of the stars for more than 370,000 years. Diodorus Siculus claimed that their observation of the stars spanned a period of 473,000 years. Thomas Taylor said the Epigenes, Berosus and Critodemes set the duration of the astronomical observations by the Babylonians at from 490,000 to 720,000 years. The history of the ancient world prepared by the Mother Church has caused us to regard the ancient Greeks as leaders in the science of antiquity. But the Greeks themselves admitted that all of their greatest scientists, philosophers and astrologers went to Egypt and Babylon to acquire their learning. In those remote days it was tacitly understood that the astrologers and mathematicians knew that the Earth is spherical and orbited the sun in an easterly direction, and also that the sun is the center of this planetary system, which is but a minute particle rotating around the Central Fire.

That was some of the ancient knowledge destroyed by the Mother Church when it plunged the great Roman Empire into the Dark Ages in order to make people believe in its wild claims and base dogmas.

And millions of stupid, mind-conditioned people still believe in what they are taught to hold them in line. But the number is rapidly decreasing, due to the acquisition and dissemination of knowledge.

A recent issue of a certain religious publication, worried about the future of Christianity, said that only one in twelve persons in America attend Church, and that seven out of eight children quit Church and Sunday School before they reach the age of 15.

There are many evils also in our educational system. It is gripped tightly in the clutch of vicious materialism, medicalism, and religiousism. And those who are at the head of the large educational organizations are also in the clutch of these sordid ISMS.

Above all else, the unthinking people are groping in the dark, due to mind-conditioning. And that is the chief purpose and design of the educational systems, which are controlled by these avaricious ISMS, as we have shown in our work titled *The Golden Dawn.*

Chapter No. 3 – Magic Esotericism

"The reason why Bible students have been deceived is because they have studied this concocted 'Word of God' instead of the WORK OF GOD" (Krypton, in *Quartum Organum*, p. 457).

Before the Mother Church burned the ancient libraries and destroyed the ancient scrolls to conceal the Ageless Wisdom of the Ancient Maki, it prepared its Bible, the "Word of God" doing the work in such a clever manner that we defy any one to read one paragraph in that Word of God and find in it either fact or fraud stated separately. Each falsity is inseparably linked with an undeniable fact, and the fact and the falsity are so intricately and delicately interwoven, that it is absolutely impossible for the unprepared mind to separate the one from the other.

This book has gone out to the world and chained in darkness and ignorance a larger number of people than any other secular book has ever done, and those victims must live in that error until they evolve to such mental ability that they can winnow the fact from the false in this book and come to understand its falseness.

We will quote a line to illustrate the skillful manner in which the work was done: "The testimony of Jesus is the spirit of prophecy" (Rev. 19:10). In the ancient scrolls that line said: "The evidence of resurrection is the power of seership." The subject being discussed in that case was the raising of the creative essence from the spinal base to the brain, in order to increase man's consciousness and lift him up to a higher level, as explained in our work titled *"Awaken The World Within."*

We stated in another place that the Bible speaks in words with a triple meaning. That meaning includes the literal, the symbolical, and the esoteric. That's the reason why the Esoteric and the Exoteric derive different meanings from the same words. The Esoteric see the Processes of Creation, whereas the Exoteric see the Products of Creation. The Esoteric learn how the work is done, but the Exoteric learn nothing in that respect. The Esoteric know the work is performed by definite Cosmic Creative Principles; but the Exoteric think it is done by a mysterious God.

To the Esoteric there is no mystery in creative work; but to the Exoteric all is mystery. To the Esoteric the realm of Knowledge is a clear field; but to the Exoteric everything is enveloped in fog. And so, the Esoteric march boldly onward, knowing where they are going and what to expect, but the Exoteric wander in darkness and are fearful of what will happen next.

This state of fog and darkness in which the Exoteric live, is largely the work of religion and the priesthood, and is designed to keep the masses in darkness and make them obedient slaves. In order to give the Exoteric a glimpse of biblical teaching understood by the Esoteric, we will cite the passage which says:

"In the midst of the throne, and round about the throne, were four beests full of eyes before and behind. And the first beast was like a lion, and the second beast like a calf, and the third beast had a face as a man, and the fourth beast was like a flying eagle' (Rev. 4:6,7). This message refers to the four fixed signs of the ancient symbol called the Zodiac. (1) Leo (Lion), (2) Taurus (Bull-calf), (3) Aquarius (Man, Water Bearer), and (4) Scorpio (Eagle).

These four signs signify the Four Elements of the Creative Principle, Fire, Earth, Water, Air, constituted of atoms "full of eyes before and behind."

The Ancient Magi, in their search for Knowledge, studied Creation, and founded their philosophy of Creation on the postulate of a fourfold elemental basis. And this basis of the Universe appears on each level of integration in a different guise, to-wit:

1.   The element traditionally called Fire appeared as Adventivity.

2.   The element traditionally called Air appeared as Reason.

3.   The element traditionally called Water appeared as Emotion.

4.   The element traditionally called Earth appeared as Will.

It may seem to the Exoteric that to try to connect human consciousness with Cosmic Cycles is a farce. Likewise, it may seem the height of absurdity to assure that the qualities of inspiration, emotion, reason and will could have anything to do with the qualities manifested on other levels. Yet there is no valid reason for denying the actuality of this state of affairs, simply because we cannot directly and intuitively perceive these affinities. We must never forget that Man, the Microcosm, is a miniature Universe.

And that is just one example of the Hidden Knowledge presented all thru the Bible, clarity to the Esoteric and confusion to the Exoteric, designed that way by the Ancient Magi. For the Exoteric, the work of finding traces of Hidden Knowledge ends in failure. On every occasion an investigator comes upon the attempt to express in one way or another the content of Hidden Knowledge, he invariably finds the same thing, namely, the poverty of human imagination in the face of this concept.

In the fairy-tales of all periods and people, adults get lost when confronted with the question of what they want and would like to have. They are unable to determine and formulate their wish. They remember only some unimportant desire, or they express several contradictory wishes, which cancel one another, or else they are unable to keep within the bounds of possible things, and, always wishing for more and more, they wind up by attempting to subjugate higher force, not being conscious of the poverty of their own powers and capacities. In the biblical legend of Solomon, appears an explanation of these tales, an explanation of what it is that men can receive if they only know what to wish for. We quote:

"In Gibeon the Lord appeared to Solomon in a dream by night, and God said, Ask what I shall give thee. ... And Solomon said ... I am but a little child, and I know not how to go out or to come in. And thy servant is in the midst of thy people. ... Give therefore thy servant an UNDERSTANDING HEART to judge thy people, that I may discern between good and bad.

"And the speech pleased the Lord that Solomon had ask this thing. And God said unto him, Because thou hast asked this thing and hast not asked for thyself long life; neither hast asked riches for thyself, nor hast asked the life of thine enemies, but has asked for thyself UNDERSTANDING. ... Behold, I have done according to thy words; lo, I have given thee a WISE AND UNDERSTANDING HEART (Mind); so that there was none like thee before thee, neither after thee shall any arise like unto thee. And I have also given thee that which thou hast not asked, both riches and honor. ... and I will lengthen thy days" (1 Kings, 3:5-15).

It would anger a modern adult to tell him he is but a little child, and knows not how to go out or to come in. It would insult an arrogant scientist to tell him those things. And yet he is in the same boat you are, and is searching for the same things you are. His science is founded on assumptions and speculations, and changes with the wind, as new thoughts and new discoveries shatter his pet assumptions and cherished speculations. That he calls "progress."

Man is conscious of being surrounded by a wall concealing the Unknown. He believes he can pierce that wall, but he cannot determine what he may find behind it. He does not even know what he would like to find behind it, or what it means to have knowledge of the mystery behind that wall.

In the history of human thought there are numerous attempts to define the limit of possible knowledge. But there are no attempts to conceive what the extension of these limits would mean and where it would lead. Science asserts that nothing is impossible; and everything is certain within the limits of that possibility.

The work of Creation is an open book and never changes. But man is unable to read with understanding what appears right before his eyes. Man plants an apple seed in the ground, and it grows and in time an apple tree comes into existence, and produces fruit. He knows when he plants the seed what the result will be. He is a prophet because he knows that much about the laws of Creation. To one who knows less, he appears as a God. And that work of Creation has been an open book before the eyes of man, yet what he beholds is too simple, too magical, too mysterious for him to understand.

Science cannot duplicate any of the simple creative processes that produce trees and seeds. Then it moves up much higher and is so arrogant as to claim that it can make a poison called medicine that will get a sick body well. And it does not even know why the body is sick. This is another great field of fraud. But it is highly profitable and drags in the dollars. The power that grows trees and seeds also produces the human body, and it is the only power that can get a sick body well.

That great discovery we made during the years we operated a sanitarium. Most of our patients came to us after the scientific medics had given them up to die. We wisely turned them over to the power that produces trees, seeds and people. And they all recovered as if by magic, and went home happy. We never lost a case.

Our patients could not understand it. They thought we employed some secret form of magic. And so we did. But it was the same magic that produces trees, seeds, and people. This magic work of Creation is what religion calls the work of God, and pushes the problem back in a corner and considers the mystery solved. That's the way the world is taught to solve the secrets of Creation.

That course solves nothing. It causes confusion and leaves man in darkness and ignorance. That builds the world of exploitation, in which live and thrive the base institutions that profit on the miseries of man. That builds the grand world called Civilization.

Chapter No. 4 – Magic & Mystery

"The word Magic is derived from the Chaldean word Maghdim, which means WISDOM, with the addition of the general sense that we give to the term PHILOSOPHY" (Jean Baptiste, in *History & Practice of Magic,* 1870, p. 18).

We live in a world of Magic and Mystery. We live in a world of ignorance and darkness. We are mind-conditioned and brain-washed to keep us in ignorance and darkness in order to make us peaceful victims of a world of fraud.

What is Life? What is Death? What are we? Whence did we come? Why are we here? Whither do we go?

The modern world looks to its mechanical god — science — for answers to these questions, and the people look to medical science to save them from sickness. And the scientists are searching for the same things the people are, and the medics suffer from the same sickness that afflicts their patients.

When we search the books for knowledge on the leading questions that fill our mind, we find the books are written to record the assumptions and speculations of the scientists and the doctors, of the philosophers and the preachers, and these assumptions and speculations are subject to change with the shifting of the wind. Let us turn to living nature and consider the magic work of Creative Action. We find that propagation is the result of cellular fission. A little cell splits and becomes two halves, and the halves keep dividing again and again without end. With each division the number of cells doubles.

This is the fixed and regular process of propagation in the living world. Propagation starts with a single cell, the bearer of the new product. And within the cell are the instructions which direct the cells in their mysterious work of building the various products of living nature.

As if by magic, every spring buds form on the trees, green shoots appear, and develop into leaves and flowers. With unerring consistency Creation snips out the petals of pansies, asters, and daisies into their fanciful forms and various colors, and binds rosebuds into tight knots. Autumn comes, and fruits ripen from the flowers. Within each fruit there is a tiny cell that carries the detailed program of Life.

Then Spring comes, the sunshine grows warmer, and the heat causes the seeds to sprout and turn again into delicate bluebells, the spear-like ears of wheat or the strong tubular stalks of maize—inimitable, intricate living structures which constantly repeat themselves from generation to generation.

How does Creation cram so much knowledge into a microscopic cell? How does it code its program for building the intricate adult organism? Science does not know.

The cell can be regarded as a factory, in which the nucleus is the executive branch, which issues the orders as to production. The information needed for the factory to operate—blueprints, templates, production-plans, all are stored away in coiled strands of molecules. The production shops, with the machinery, and the workers responsible for output, are situated in the cytoplasm, the fluid filling the cells.

Such magic; such mystery; inimitable and infallible; the common course of Creative Action; so simple yet so stupefying. These magical methods of Creation appear baffling to us. Our intelligence does not encounter itself in the mysterious work of Creative Activity. We cannot understand the mode of organization of our body and its nutritive, nervous, and mental activities. The illusions of the mechanicists of the 19th Century, the dogmas of Jacques Loeb, and the childish physio-chemical conception of man, in which physiologists and physicians believe, should be definitely abandoned because they are utterly erroneous.

And that is what medical science knows about man and the magical work of building him, and the mysterious functions of his body. They don't know the actual cause of sickness, and think the body is unable to run its own business, making it necessary for doctors to move in with their poisons falsely called medicine. And all patients who recover under their care do so in spite of them and not because of them.

For at least a century, science has been elevated to the status of a religion. "Genesis is not in it with a school text-book on chemistry," said Prof. J. H. Woodger. This scientific dogmatism dates from the days of our grandfathers, who imagined the Universe as a huge machine made of hard, indivisible atoms. Thinking was a vibration of the molecules in the brain Consciousness was an "epiphenomenon." Everything progressed under the impact of the mechanical forces of evolution.

Due to the splitting of the atom, the progress of science has now reached a turning point. The stable foundations of physics have broken up. The old foundations of scientific thought are becoming unintelligible. Time, space, matter, mineral, ether, electricity, mechanism, organism, configuration, structure, pattern, function, all require reinterpretation. What is the sense of talking about a mechanical explanation when you don't know what you mean by mechanics?

In referring to the magic work of Creation in the production of a human being, Sir Charles Sherrington said: "The germ-cells can be likened crudely enough to a set of magic bricks. The original fertilized cell divides into two, and so on. When that process has gone on in the aggregate some fifty-five times, there are twenty-six million million magic bricks instead of one. That is about the number in the human child at birth.

"These cells have arranged themselves into a complex which is a human child. Each cell in all that more than million-fold population has taken up its right position. Each cell has assumed its required form and size in the right place. Each cell has taken on the shape which will suit its particular business in the cell-community of which it is a member, whether its skill is to lie in mechanical pulling, chemical manufacture, gas-transport, radiation-absorption, or what not. More still, it has done so as though it knew the minute local conditions of the particular spot in which its lot is east" (*Man and His Nature*).

Science delights in picturing the human body as being constructed like one of our machines. A machine is composed of many parts. The body originates from a single cell, and builds itself. The machine wears out with use, but the body improves with use and deteriorates from non-use. And it cannot grow old, for it is constantly rebuilding and renewing all of its parts, down to the biggest bone, and is never more than seven years old. For this reason, science claims that man should live forever.

Another strange factor is that isolated cells possess intelligence and have the singular power of reproducing, without direction or purpose, the edifices characterizing each organ.

If a few red corpuscles, impelled by gravity, flow horn a drop of blood placed in liquid plasma and form a tiny stream, banks are soon built up. Then, these banks cover themselves with filaments of fibrin, and the stream becomes a pipe, thru which the red cells glide just as in a blood vessel.

Cells exhibit intelligence like bees do in erecting their geometrical alveoli, synthetizing honey, feeding their embryos, as tho each one of them understood mathematics, chemistry, and biology, and unselfishly acted for the benefit of the entire community. The spontaneous tendency toward the formation of the organs by their constitutive cells, like the social aptitude of the insects, is a primary datum of observation; and it cannot be explained in the light of our present knowledge.

An organ builds itself by techniques very foreign to the human mind. It is not made of extraneous material, like a house. Neither is it a cellular construction, a mere assemblage of cells. It is, of course, composed of cells, as a house is composed of bricks. But it is born from a cell, as if the house originated from one brick, a magic brick that would set about manufacturing more bricks out of itself.

Those magic bricks, without waiting for the architect's drawings or the coming of the bricklayers, would assemble themselves and form the walls. They would also metamorphose into windowpanes, roofing-slate, coal for heating, and water for the kitchen and bathroom.

An organ develops by magical means such as those attributed to fairies in the tales told to children. It is engendered by cells which, to all appearances, have knowledge of the future edifice, and synthesize from substances contained in the blood plasma the building material and even the workers.

Creation performs many marvellous transformations that amaze and astound. For example, if a person had never seen it nor been told about it, he could never imagine that an offensive-looking little caterpillar would change into a beautiful butterfly. Yet we know by experience this is what occurs.

It is also just as amazing that little seeds planted in the ground produce red beets, green beans, white onions, yellow corn, water-melons, apple trees, etc. The Ancient Magi had answers and symbols for everything in the world of Creation. With the interlaced triangles, they symbolized Creative Activity as a dual process of operation. This may be called involution and evolution, and it goes on simultaneously.

Perhaps we can understand this better by visualizing two great arcs. The one of Matter is called the shadowy or descending part, for downward it slowly spirals all the hosts of entities as they automatically clad themselves in ever denser garments (coats of skins—Pen. 3:21), until they reach the lowest extremity of Matter existing on the lowest plane of the earth. Then in the reverse process (evolution) the various life-waves of solar sparks start to climb up the arc of the celestial — the Luminous or Ascending Arc. And on that upward journey they begin to shed their denser garments in exchange for the finer vestments of the empyreal realm. Creation does not operate by leaps and bounds, nor does it skip any steps or leave any gaps.

With infinite action, Creation works with but one purpose in view, and that is to produce thru repetition, in cycle after cycle, the full potential of its production. And that includes every group of living things which inhabit the universe—from the smallest speck of electronic matter, thru all the various kingdoms, on up to the loftiest divinities functioning in and behind the supergalactic systems.

Worlds are organisms of their kind. For the creation of so vast an organism, consciousness must have energy proportionate to its task. This is derived from the latent but incalculable source called space. Creative energy is this latent energy organized and intelligized by genetic ideation (consciousness).

This in Involution, or Cosmogenesis. In order that epigenetic consciousness may be achieved, the genetic creates the biologic organism. This is Evolution, or Biogenesis. Consciousness, energy and organism are the three essentials of being. The first two are cause; the third, effect. The first two are mutually interdependent. Neither consciousness alone nor energy alone can accomplish anything creative.

There are just two definite Principles in the entire universe—consciousness and energy. Consciousness must be empowered by energy, and energy must be directed by consciousness.

These two Principles are inextricably united thruout the whole creative process. Due to this fact, we might term them energized consciousness, or consciousized energy. Whatever we term them, they are the eternal aspect of the Creative Triad. And whatever qualities we ascribe to them, they are but planetary genetics.

Chapter No. 5 – Magic Creation

"The body is engendered by cells which, to all appearances, have knowledge of the future edifice, and synthetize from substances contained in the blood plasma the building material and even the builders" (Dr. Alexis Carrel, in *Man the Unknown*).

The mysterious operation of Creative Activity is magic. Something seem to come forth from nothing. Like a little seed producing a tree, or an invisible speck producing a person. Nothing any one can imagine could be more magical than the creation of man, the king of the earth. It was the magical work of Creation that attracted the attention of the Ancient Magi. They devoted deep study to these mysteries, and from their discoveries they developed their Ageless Wisdom.

Magic in general has been confounded too long with spurious jugglery and deceptive mountebanks, the hallucinations of disordered minds, and the crimes of unusual malefactors.

Magic is not to be represented as this or that by any person whomsoever. For Magic is the exact and absolute science of Creation and its laws. Magic combines in a single body that which is certain in philosophy, which is eternal in science, and infallible in religion. It reconciles perfectly and simplifies incontestably those terms, so opposed on the first view — faith and reason, science and belief, authority and wisdom.

Magic furnishes the human mind with an instrument of philosophical, theological and scientific certitude as exact as mathematics, and even accounting for the infallibility of mathematics themselves.

An Absolute does exist in the realm of reason and understanding. The light of human intelligence has not been left by the Supreme Power to waver at hazard. There is a definite truth; there is an infallible method of knowing that truth; and those who attain that knowledge, and adopt it as a rule of life, can endow their Will with a sovereign power that makes them masters of all inferior things, all wandering spirits, or, in other words, arbiters and kings of the world. If such be the case, how comes it that such an exalted science is still unrecognized. How is it possible to assume that so bright a light is hidden in a cloud so dark?

The transcendental science has been known always, but only to the flowers of intelligence, who have known the necessity of silence in practice. If a skillful surgeon, at midnight, should put sight in the eyes of a man born blind, it would still be impossible to make him realize the nature or existence of daylight until morning arrived. Science has its nights and its mornings, for the life which it communicates to the world of mind is characterized by regular modes of motion and progressive phases.

It is the same with the truth as it is with the radiation of light. Nothing which is hidden is lost. But at the same time nothing that is found is absolutely new. The seal of eternity is affixed by Creation to that science which is the reflection of its glory. The transcendental science, the absolute science, is assuredly Magic, yet the affirmation may seem utterly paradoxical to those who have never questioned the infallibility of Voltaire. Magic was the science of Abraham and Orpheus, of Confucius and Zoroaster. And it was Magical Doctrines which were graven on tables of stone by Enoch and by Hermes. Moses purified and re-veiled them—this being the sense of the word "revealed."

The new disguise which Moses gave them was that of the Holy Kabalah—that exclusive heritage of Israel and the inviolable secret of its priests.

The Ancient Mysteries of Thebes in Egypt and of Eleusis in Greece preserved among the Gentiles some of its mystic symbols, but in a debased form; and the mystic key was lost amidst the tangled and complicated superstition that was developing. Jerusalem, murderer of its prophets, and prostituted over and over again by false Assyrian and Babylonian gods, ended by losing in its turn the mysterious Sacred Word.

The mythical history of Freemasonry informs us that there once existed a WORD of surpassing value, and claiming a profound veneration: that this Word was known to but few; that it was eventually lost and that a temporary substitute for it was adopted. The Lost Word consisted of SEVEN LETTERS and is especially mentioned in the Bible. We have revealed it in our work titled "*The Hidden Creator.*"

It is this secret that the erudite and ill-starred Charles Dupuis should have found in the Hindu planispheres and in tables in Denderah of Egypt. He would not have ended by rejecting the truly universal and eternal philosophy in the presence of the unanimous affirmation of all Nature, as well as all monuments of science throughout the ages. It was the memory of this scientific and theological doctrine, summarized in a WORD, alternately lost and found, which was secretly transmitted to the elect of all antique initiations. Whether preserved or profaned in the celebrated Order, of the Temple, it was this sane memory, passed on to secret associations of Rosicrucians, Illuminati and Freemasons, which gave meaning to their strange rites, to their more or less conventional signs, and a justification above all to their devotion in common, as well as a clue to their power.

Dupuis attempted to explain not only all the mysteries of antiquity, but also the origin of all religious beliefs. In his book he maintained a common origin for the astronomical and theological opinions of the Greeks, Egyptians, Persians, Arabians, and Chinese. And the facts of history, when sifted out of the chaff, appear to indicate that he was right.

That profanation has befallen the doctrines and the mysteries of Ancient Magic, we have no intention to deny. That was the special work of the Mother Church. And repeated from age to age, the misuse itself has been a hard lesson for those who made unwisely known to the gullible masses the secrets of the Ancient Magi. Even our own writings in this sacred field bring only smile and scorn from most of the orthodox.

The Gnostics caused the Gnosis to be prohibited by Christians, and the official sanctuary was closed to high initiation. The hierarchy of knowledge was thus compromised by the intervention of usurping ignorance, while the disorder within the sanctuary was reproduced in the state. For, willingly or otherwise, the king always depended on the priest; and it is toward the eternal adytum of divine instruction that earthly power will ever look for consecration and for energy to insure their permanence.

The Key of Ancient Magic has been thrown to the children, symbolically speaking. And as might have been expected, it is now mislaid and practically lost. This notwithstanding, a man of high intuition and great moral courage, Count Joseph de Maistre, acknowledging that the world was void of religion and could not so remain, turned his eyes instinctively toward the last sanctuaries of occultism and called, with heartfelt prayers, for that day when the natural affinity which subsists between science and religion, should combine them in the mind of a single man of genius.

He said: "That will be grand. It will finish the eighteenth century which is still with us. ... We shall talk then of our present stupidity as we now dilate on the barbarism of the Middle Ages."

Genius is not needed to see the sun, and it has never demonstrated anything but its rare greatness and its lights inaccessible to the common crowd.

The Eternal Truth demands only to be found and recognized, and then the simplest will be able to comprehend it and to prove it also at need. At the same time, that Truth will never become vulgar, because it is hierarchic, and because anarchy alone humors the bias of the crowd.

The student should now read our folio titled "*Land of Light*," and see how cleverly the Ancient Magi symbolized the magic work of creation in the 22 Tarot Arcana.

Chapter No. 6 – Magic Message

"The existence of finality within the living organism is undeniable. Each part of the body seems to know the present and future needs of the whole, and acts accordingly. The significance of time and space is not the same for our tissues as for our mind. The body perceives the remote as well as the near, the future as well as the present" (Dr. Alexis Carrel, in *Man The Unknown*, p. 197).

Magic Message, Cosmic Consciousness, Eternal knowledge—name it and take it; examine it and describe it; study it and say what it is. Carrel knew much more about the body, about man, about life, about intelligence, than perhaps any other orthodox medic of this century. He recognized the things we mentioned in previous chapters relative to the strange intelligence and conduct manifested by the cells of the body, and logically inferred that the cells were governed by Eternal Knowledge from the cosmic source.

The Magic Message operates and governs all involuntary functions of the human temple, and the conduct of all living things below man in the scale of evolution. Science calls it Blind Instinct, and knows not what the term means. Man, referred to as the lord of the whole earth in the Bible (Zech. 4:14), with dominion over all living things (Gen. 1:26), was released from control of Eternal Knowledge by endowment of the power of Free Will, the purpose of which was to permit him to rise above the beastilic plane, and be released from suffering the regular sacrifice involved in propagation, like the helpless flowers of the field and the dumb brutes of the forest. In a previous chapter we said that when the tri-colored fire of the propagative centers at the spinal base, ascends to the brain, it endues man with mental powers of almost unlimited scope.

But the very first man, according to the Bible, failed to take advantage of this liberation. He chose the other path, and suffered the consequences. He ate the forbidden fruit (Gen. 2:17). He disgraced the generative function. He indulged in fornication for pleasure instead of for propagation, and sank in the mire of degeneration and premature death, as expounded in our work titled *"The Great Red Dragon,"* and covered more fully in our great correspondence course of 85 lessons, written forty years ago, titled Secret of Regeneration. A man of 80 is rare, a man of 90 is a wonder, and a man of 100 is almost a miracle. We are in our 91st year, with good prospects of passing the century mark, and this evidence indicates that we have lived closer to the provisions of the laws of Creation than most people do.

For years we've experienced a strange mental state that we've never mentioned in our writings. Now that mystery has been referred to by two unique authors whose remarkable writings we've read with intense interest. One of these men calls himself Phyhlotus. He wrote a rare folio titled *Esoteric Masonry*. As we are a Mason of the Knights Templar degree, we exceptionally interested in his interpretation of certain biblical allegories in relation to Masonry. Then he decided to expound hag he was able to do it. This is what he said: "Some powerful influence seers to overshadow me when I write, and from out of the unseen transfers to my mind those things which are desired that I should write.

"For a short time I was in Los Angeles, but moved out to the Sierras, and am now writing way up in the mountains, 125 miles from a town of any importance, and 23 miles from the nearest railroad point.

"I've never in my life had an instructor in the flesh as to these things. I've never seen a Mahatma, Adept, or Master of Occult Science, yet have been deeply interested in these things. I know nothing of hypnotism, mesmerism, or mediumship, and have not the least psychic power of which I'm aware. I only know that I am impelled by a strong desire to write, and yielding to this impulse, there flows into my mind the information which is to be transmitted."

So much for what Phyhlotus had to say relative to this peculiar mental state in his case. Now for the other author who said of himself:

"I do not claim to be a prophet. The ideas—mental images— about which I write, core to my mind by well-established, scientific manifestation of extra-sensory perception—of inspiration—generally after my morning meditation—in an instantaneous flash, wholly formed and coherent in thought. The thought does not originate in my third dimensional mind, but in the higher fourth dimension. I cannot claim it as my own. My problem is to reduce the concept to writing.

"I can honestly say that during my many years of controversial writing to expose the forces of corruption and disaster, I've never presented any such writings which have been in error in principle, although errors do creep in thru reproduction. There is nothing mysterious about this. A creative artist, or musician, or an Einstein, composes in much the same way, from inspiration received from the higher fourth dimension of cosmic vibration, a process fully scientific.

"A significant point arises from this technique or inspirational writing—the TRUTH flowing from that higher dimension is absolute, not relative as in our ordinary third dimensional world. It has the same power whether open or a million proclaim it. The TRUTH already and eternally exists, and needs only to be touched and revealed."

And now we shall quote what another wise man said about Truth:

"Absolute Truth is an attribute of Infinity, and is not to be found in the physical world of form, where every condition or object is modified or balanced by its direct opposite. Without this equilibrium, a physical world could not exist. The human race has made a continuous and sustained effort to upset and combat the balance of Nature in every way possible. Every law of health, every law of decency, morality, and justice has been violated by the people, and still they hope to escape payment of the penalty. These are the "Destroyers Of The Earth" mentioned in the Bible.'

Hard words but decidedly factual. In the matter of knowledge, we should realize that Eternal Knowledge had no beginning, and needs only to be touched and revealed. The Bible refers to Eternal Knowledge in these words:

"The thing that hath been, it is that which shall be (again); and that which is done is that which shall be done (again); and there is no new thing under the sun. Is there anything whereof it may be said, See, that is new? It hath been already of old tire, which was before us" (Eccl. 1:9,10).

Time and space, beginnings and endings, are illusions of the mind. There was no beginning and there can be no ending.

Eternal Knowledge has existed always. Consider the bees; they have always known how to make honey without having been taught. Bugs, birds and beasts are guided thru life by the Magic Message, Cosmic Consciousness, Eternal Knowledge. A materialistic science stupidly calls this Blind Instinct, pushes the problem back into a corner and the world considers it solved. The gullible masses think science has solved the mysteries of the Universe, and it has actually solved nothing. Our weak powers of perception reach only the fringe of Eternal Knowledge. Some can contact more than others, due to the better condition of their brain and nerves. The Ancient Magi could reach deeply into this realm because their whole body was in much better shape than ours. They did not live in a poisoned world as we do.

This is a strange department of Creation, about which material science knows practically nothing. Esoteric wisdom has gone far in this field, and examined the human temple to learn what organs respond to the vibrations from the realm of Eternal Knowledge. Those organs are centered in the Five Magic chambers of the skull. That is the Throne of the Intellectual Divinity in man, situated in the Golden Bowl (Eccl. 12:6). This is a highly important subject and we have noticed it more fully in another chapter.

It has now come to pass that we, in our 91st year, shall reveal a personal secret that we've never published before. We do not claim to possess Spiritual Vision; but there is something strange about the proposition that we do not understand. We tell our story chiefly because of the confessions made by the two authors mentioned, relative to how their strange knowledge is received by them.

We've been a professional writer for half a century, and our writings circle the globe. Many of our readers regard us as an exceptional person because of the strange things mentioned in our writings.

We shall try to reveal the peculiar manner in which this knowledge comes to us. And it is not ours; it belongs to the world, as it were. It is difficult to put into words the strange form in which we receive this knowledge. It occurs when we are deep in the land of dreams, and our body is unconscious in sleep. This may be called dreaming. What is dreaming?

The knowledge we desire about a certain subject on which we have thought and studied during several days, comes to us when we are in dreamland. And the way in which it comes is also strange. It comes in books, in books written by unknown hands, in books written by the Ancient Magi.

The books appear before us as if by magic, as if given to us by an unseen spirit. And we read them while our body is unconscious in sleep. And the words, as we read them, appear so strangely. We see no line of words, but just one word at a time. As we read each word, that word vanishes in a flash, and its place is taken in a flash by the next word. And so on all thru the trance. The words disappear as we read them, and the next word flashes before us, one at a time, as if some magic power were operating the process.

As soon as we awaken, we get up and write down the messages while they are fresh in our mind, otherwise we would lose them and be unable to recall them. Sometimes these events fail to awaken us, and then the messages are gone, lost, and we cannot recover them.

One of the above authors expounded the mystery by claiming the knowledge comes from the higher, fourth dimension of cosmic vibrations, a process fully scientific, he said. And coming from the higher dimension, the knowledge is absolute and not relative, as in the common third dimension world.

There is another angle of the mystery that should be noticed. For instance, we can take the juice out of a lemon, but we cannot take the lemon out of the juice; for the juice is the substance of the lemon.

This law has no exceptions, and under this law the process of Creation can take man out of the Creator, but cannot take the Creator out of the man; for man is the Substance of the Creator, and the biblical statement is literally correct when it says the Kingdom of God is within you (Lu. 17:21).

And God is in his kingdom as expounded in our work titled *"The Hidden Creator."*

Emerson referred to this mystery when he wrote:

"The true doctrine of omnipresence means that the Creator appears in every moss and every cobweb. ... The world is not the product of manifold powers, but of One Power, of One Will, of One Mind; and the Universal One is active everywhere, in each Ray of the Star and in each wavelet of the pool."

The realization of this cosmic state awakens in man's mind the realm of Eternal Knowledge, and it becomes operative when not retarded by the Five Senses which make man a prisoner in his temple. But the higher function is so rare as to be practically unknown, and so mysterious as to be beyond the common comprehension.

It may be well to tell another story of what we did as a boy 9, 10 and 11 years old.

We were not only a dreamer, but also a sleep-walker, a somnambulist. We would get out of bed in the night, in our sleep, put on our clothes, and walk about the house—go to the kitchen and get a drink of water; go to the cupboard and get something to eat; go to the outside door, unlock it, open it and go outside. Our parents had to watch us, and jump out of bed and grab us, wake us up, and make us go back to bed.

We did no more of that after we were 12 years old. We were most active in that respect during our 10th and 11th years. When man is in a trance, or unconscious in sleep, or from injury, the five tricky senses that block the operation of Eternal Knowledge are blacked-out, thus permitting the Magic Message to operate unrestricted. This is what the gospel Jesus referred to when he said: *"For there is nothing covered that shall not be revealed, nor hid, that shall not be known"* (Mat. 10:26).

Chapter No. 7 – Magic Spirit

"You are a child of the Universal Creative Spirit. You are a Spark of Divine Fire, manifesting in a material body. You are a God in a form of Flesh. ... Your real being is the Creator within you. When you think, I'm God in human form, you mean that you are looking within; and then you learn that you cannot die. For the God within you is your Life" (*Light of The Universe*, p. 4).

Material science does not agree with the sentiment presented in the above quotation. It claims there is no definite Life Principle. It holds that the Life manifested by the organism is just body function, resulting from chemical action and reaction within the body's cells and tissues.

When body function ceases for any reason, the lifeless organism, in due time, disintegrates, decays, and returns to dust, like a log of wood. And that, according to the postulate of science, is the finality of man.

That hypothesis of material science falls far short of a satisfactory solution of the mystery of Life. It considers only the physical body, and fails to agree with the regular facts of axial observation. Science does not consider that before chemical changes could occur within the body, some definite power besides chemistry would have to produce the body. Wm. Osler, said to have been the greatest physician this country ever produced, denied the existence of Life as a principle. He wrote:

"Life is (just) the expression of a series of chemical changes (within the body)" (Modern Med., p. 39).

Many facts of common observation must be ignored to believe in Osler's statement. Life must be more than the effect of the chemical changes of matter. Matter possesses no power of itself to create man as a living being. Science moves in a circle when it holds that Life is the effect of Chemical changes in matter, and these changes are Life. A satisfactory definition of Life must comprehend the element attested. It must determine the CAUSE of these chemical changes, or else it is not a definition of Life, but merely a description of the effects produced in matter by an unknown cause.

The great scientist of this century, Dr. Alexis Carrel, made a deep study of Life and Man. This is the conclusion he reached: "A mechanistic physiologist and a vitalistic physiologist do not consider the organism in the same light. The living being of Jacques Loeb differs profoundly from that of Hans Driesch. Indeed, mankind has made a gigantic effort to know itself. ... each one of us is made up of a procession of phantoms, in the midst of which there strides an unknowable reality" (*Man The Unknown*, 1935, p. 4).

For an orthodox scientist, Carrel made a surprising statement. He refused to regard the medical theory as to Life and man. He considered man as a dual being. No other orthodox scientist known to us has ever viewed men in that light, and we've been reading their books for seventy years in our searching's to solve the mystery of the Magic Being called Man. We notice that Carrel made no definite attempt to identify the duality of man that he mentioned. His "procession of phantoms" is the only part orthodox science ever considers. That is the whole man according to the hypothesis of science. Carrel's "unknowable reality" it refuses to recognize. In the mystery of Life, Carrel knew that science is lost in a fog. He said:

"Those (scientists) who investigate the phenomena of Life are as if lost in an inextricable jungle, in the midst of a magic forest, whose countless trees unceasingly change their place and their shape" (*Man The Unknown*, p. 1).

When men grope in darkness as described by Carrel, they are ignoramuses posing as scientists. The books they write and the statements they make are too unreliable to receive serious attention. And these are the books studied by students in universities and medical colleges. Such are the books on which is based the education of the medics. And where do we go from here? Back to the Bible; we have no other choice.

The mystery before us was considered by the Apostle Paul in the 15th chapter of his first Epistle to the Corinthians, which is considered by many learned men to mark the high point of spiritual sublimity in the New Testament. Paul regarded man as a dual being just as Carrel did. But he seemed to be wiser in that field than Carrel was. He went on and defined Carrel's "procession of phantoms" and his "unknowable reality." This is what he said:

"The first man (procession of phantoms) is of the earth, earthy; and the second man (unknowable reality) is the LORD FROM HEAVEN" (1 Cor. 15:47). Paul's identification of the Unknowable Reality may surprise the reader. It went right to the heart of the mystery of Life and the enigma of Spiritual Man.

We are still in the shadows of mystery. What had Paul in mind when he mentioned the LORD FROM HEAVEN? Let us follow him further and see. In another place he said:

"For what man knoweth the things of a man, save the spirit of man which is in him; even so the things of God knoweth no man, but the spirit of God (within). ... Know ye not that ye are the temple of God, and that the Spirit of God dwelleth in you? If any man defile the temple of God, him shall God destroy; for the temple of God is holy, which temple ye are. ... What? Know ye not that your body is the temple of the Holy Ghost which is in you, which ye have of God, and ye are not your own" (1 Cor. 2:11; 3:16, 17; 6:19, 20).

In this description of the mystery, it appears that Paul attempted to tell the world what the Bible means when it says, the Kingdom of God is within you (Luke 17:21).

Science would never stoop so low as to consider anything presented in the scriptures of the superstitious heathens of antiquity. But we have no other choice. We must follow the Bible or admit the mystery before us is unsolvable. It is well to consider next what the great Mason Albert Pike had to say in his book titled *Morals & Dogma of Freemasonry*, published in 1871. In leading up to the Kingdom of God within, this is what he wrote:

"Our senses are mysteries to us, and we are mysteries to ourselves. Philosophy has taught us nothing but words as to the nature of our sensations, our perceptions, our cognizance's, our mind, the origin of our thoughts and ideas. By no effort or degree of reflection, never so long continued, can man become conscious of a personal identity in himself, separate and distinct from his own body and brain" (p. 528).

Pike presents the surprising suggestion that Gad is in his kingdom in the form of flesh called Man, and is the eternal

Entity Paul termed the Spirit of God. Pike put more power in this point by asserting that man cannot contact within himself any other "personal identity separate and distinct from this (own) body and brain." In plainer terms, the entity the world regards as man is none other than the Spirit of God within the human temple, exactly as stated by Paul. That we have covered in our great work titled *"THE HIDDEN CREATOR"*. We must keep this fact in mind: The Spirit of God within the human temple is restricted in action by the capacities and abilities of the temple.

We must recognize the further fact that the Creator must be in his Creations during their life. For He is that Life. The demise of the created formation caned man indicates the departure there from of the Creator, the God within. The created formation of the body is visible. But the Spirit of God within the body is invisible. Paul expounded that difference in these words:

"We look not at the things which are seen, but the things which are not seen; for things which are seen are temporal, but the things which are not seen are eternal" (2, Cor. 4:18).

The Creative Force, unseen, untreated, eternal, God within, can co-exist only with a counter-force, which is the created object that can be seen. And the existence of either without the presence of the other is an impossibility. This means that when the created form dies, disintegrates and returns to dust, it has been deserted by the Spirit of God.

H. P. Blavatsky endorsed what Paul wrote when she said:

"Throughout the whole range of mystic literature of the ancient world, we detect the same idea of Spiritual Esotericism that the personal God exists only within the worshipper, and never without. That personal Deity is no vain breath, nor a fiction of the imagination, but the immortal Entity" (Secret Doctrine.)

It's surprising how stupid people can be to believe in a God who does everything and hides in seclusion and nobody knows anything about him. It's reasonable to assume that such a God does not exist except in the imagination. There is an Immortal Entity in the human temple, and that Entity, as a Ray of the Creator, is analogous to a Ray of sunlight as an individualized manifestation of the Sun.

As the Ray becomes individualized in flower and fruit, so the Animative Ray of the Creator becomes individualized in human flesh, inhabiting the form of flesh as the Ego, the Spiritual God, as the Bible says, and doing the work on the earth plane which man erroneously thinks he does.

The visible world is full of illusions, and this is one of them. They are misunderstood because of what we are taught and because our senses deceive us. We see not what we think we see. The qualities of the Creator appear in man and are a mystery to science. Some of the qualities are called vitality, consciousness, mind and intelligence. In no medical work ever written are these qualities logically described or sensibly defined.

We are assured by science that we inhabit a Universe that is destitute of life and consciousness, and is constituted of blind instinct and unknown forces. When we follow that system of science we find ourselves in a world of ignorance, where great scientists are searching for the same things for which the cannon man of darkness is searching.

Chapter No. 8 – Magic Kingdom

"All that man knows is received from his brain All that his brain knows is received from the nerves. All the nerves can transmit to the brain are the sensations produced by the environment. that is the beginning and the ending of man's knowledge" (Dr. Oliver Dahl, in Brain 8 Nerves, 1914).

In the creation of Man, King of the Earth, Creation produced an organism for his home in the visible world that was an automatic mechanism with a remarkable control unit—the brain—joined by nerves to all parts and organs of the body. This home, the human temple, is a complex cybernetic structure, controlled by countless self-regulating devices. Every single cell of the body is an automatic control center in its own right. Billions of tiny cybernetic units are constantly working within us. They maintain normal blood pressure, regulate the composition of the gastric juices, and ensure the rhythmic contraction of heart and lungs, and all things that are classified as vital function.

No doctor should ever interfere with the vital functions. For all functions, whether in health or in sickness, are always under rigid control of the cybernetic units. And they eternally work to preserve and protect the body and never to destroy it. If we remove the top of the skull, lift out of the body the brain and nerves, all that remains is a lifeless form of flesh and bone. The entire mystery of Life is contained and concealed within the brain and nerves. That is the Kingdom of God within.

When the principles of Chiropractic were discovered by accident in 1895, students of the art had to study medical textbooks because there were no others covering the subjects involved. Chiropractic deals chiefly with the nervous system; and the daily experience of the Chiropractors proved the theories and assumptions expressed in these medical books, as to the nerves and their functions, to be definitely erroneous.

And so, a committee of Chiropractors, of which the great Chiropractor, Willard Carver, was the leader, wrote their own books covering the nerves and their functions. And these books we studied when we attended Carver Chiropractic College in Oklahoma City, the first chartered Chiropractic College in the world. The books of medical science relative to the nerves and their functions show the medics know very little about that important matter. Medical science opines that all properties expressed by man result from brain and nerve function. And so they do. But medical science cannot expound how the work is done, nor describe the true nature of the force involved.

The brain has been probed, dissected, and studied by the medic's right down to its cells and atoms, and nothing has been found to account for life, consciousness, mind, intelligence, soul, spirit, etc. These mysteries take us beyond anything conventional that science has to offer.

Biologists, psychologists and physiologists all over the world have discovered and presented evidence that there is much more involved in the constitution of man and his consciousness than science suspects.

With his large brain, man, the King of the Earth, should possess knowledge in all directions far superior to that of any other living creature. And without doubt that was the case at one time. But such is not the case now. And there are reasons. One of the reasons is the mind-conditioning and brain-washing to which man is constantly subjected from early childhood until he goes to the grave. And the purpose of this clever work is to keep him in ignorance and darkness while making him believe it is for his benefit.

The essence of brain activity is the capacity to receive simultaneously the different and the rapidly altering stimulations from the external world; to translate these swiftly and accurately into terms of knowledge of the things and conditions which surround us in our environment, and to correlate these sensations and interpretations swiftly so as to transmit the orders for any necessary actions by remote parts of the body. These orders are carried by the nerves. The swifter, the more accurate, the wore capable of receiving simultaneously a multitude of impressions, and correlating them all, the higher is the intellectual capacity of the individual.

But without the nervous system, the brain would be useless. All of man's knowledge of the world comes to him thru his nerves. The vibrations and sensations of the world that affect the nerves, are transmitted to the brain by the afferent nerves called the optic, the auditory, the olfactory, the tactile, and the gustatory.

The brain receives the vibrations and sensations from the external world, and translates them into certain knowledge called seeing, hearing, smelling, feeling, and tasting. And that is the beginning and the end of man's ability to acquire knowledge of his environment and of the world. It will surprise the student if we present some reflex actions of man that are triggered by the stimulation of a single nerve cell.

Consider such a simple sensation as thirst. Depending on circumstances, a "thirst urge" will cause man to engage in a wide range of activity: Take a pail, find a well, lower the pail into it, draw up some water, etc.

If one is camping out in the open, the thirst urge ray elicits considerable effort to get a drink of water. Yet it all begins when one or two tiny cells of the brain that are sensitive to water shortage in the blood, are activated, triggering millions of other neurons into action. A single element several microns in diameter, not a big thirst center, is what activates the intricate mechanism of the brain.

One of the greatest misconceptions as to the character of our faculties of perception is that our eyes see, our ears hear, our nose smells, etc. Our sense organs are merely receptors, specifically designed to pick up stimuli or vibrations generated by the environment.

Our eyes detect electro-magnetic waves of a certain length constituting the optical region of the spectrum; the ears detect air vibrations of specific frequency and volume, but they do not see nor hear. Their task is to translate incoming signals into the language of nerve impulses and transmit them further on.

The perception of light, sound and other external stimuli occurs in the respective areas of the cerebral cortex: the visual, auditory, taste, olfactory and other areas. The body's sense organs are the brains receptors which keep man informed of events in the external world. That is the secret of how the Kingdom of God knows what's going on. The optic nerve extends from the light-sensitive retina of each eye to the visual center situated around the post lateralgytus at the back of the brain. It is designated as area 17 by the physiologists who study these matters. If this area is damaged, blindness results even tho the optic nerves are intact. ...If area 17 is stimulated, a person sees sparks or glowing spheres.

Our visual system is a complex structure, designed for the reception and transmission of images, or rather information about images. In this respect it resembles a television system, like the one that brings the images to the TV set in your home. "Television in the brain" the skeptic may say; "impossible." But man can make nothing that Creation has not been making down thru the ages. Man is just a copyist.

We lack space here to discuss the nerves of the other sense organs, but from what has been said relative to the eyes and their nerves, the reader can understand that the nervous system is a highly complicated mechanism. And that's what we encounter when we consider the Kingdom of God within.

From this basic cognition as the starting point, man proceeds by imagination, assumption and speculation to evolve his systems of science which fill the books and are taught in the schools and universities. As time, experience and new discoveries prove this and that theme to be erroneous, some are dropped and their places filled with more imagination, assumption and speculation, which time and experience may prove to be just as faulty and fantastic as those that were discarded. This continues from year to year and from century to century, and is <u>called</u> progress. But the schemes that drag in the dollars are tightly held and never rejected, no matter how faulty they may prove to be. And that is one of the ways in which has been developed the money-making systems of this world of fraud

Due to the mind-conditioning and brain-washing administered by the Institutions that control civilization, people are very stupid. Prof. Wm. James, renowned psychologist, said

"Compared with what we ought to be, we are less than half awake. We make use of only a small part of our physical and mental resources. Stating the matter broadly, man thus lives far below his level. He possesses powers of various sorts which he habitually fails to use. The result is that the nonuse of these organs causes them to lapse into a state of dormancy."

Fifty percent of the masses are almost mentally blank and do practically no thinking of their own. Twenty- five percent are partially blank. Investigation shows that the best of us use less than ten percent of our brain capacity. Matters are made worse by the fact that the Five Senses limit our knowledge and generally deceive us. And in addition to this, the mind is conditioned and controlled by education, by training, by brain-washing, by theology, by the social pattern, etc. Free the mind from these paralyzing controls, increase the scope of its perception by activating the Sixth and Seventh Sense Powers, and.Man becomes the master who directs his Destiny with what appears as supernatural powers.

Since the Microcosm is a replica of the Macrocosm, it is logical to assure that the law which governs the one also rules the other. And so, if man desires to know the laws of the Cosmos, he should study in the laboratory within himself. And if he there extracts the quintessence of his own atomic forces and harnesses them by the power of his Will, he should attain to the state which is above and beyond the merely human as known to us—he will no longer be man, but the Seer, the Superman.

There is much in the world man used to know, and should know, but does not know now because of his crippled powers of perception. That is the reason why some people know more than others, learn faster than others, live longer than others, etc. Their brain and nervous system are in better shape than others due to a better environment and a better mode of living.

It's possible to increase man's power of perception, and if it were increased ten-fold, his scope of knowledge of himself and of the world would be increased proportionately. The power of perception of the Human Temple can be vastly increased beyond what it is at present. That would require a better condition of body, brain, nerves, environment, a change in the mode of education from the instilling of darkness to that of imparting Light, the elimination of our false religious system, the recognition of God as the Animative Power within the body—in fact, a complete revamping of the very foundation of our fraudulent civilization. Of course these things and changes will never come to pass. They are the product of ages of scheming and planning, and will remain as they are. Only a few individuals here and there will silently work their way out; and they must do it secretly, or else.

The nervous system supplies the brain with all knowledge man has of himself and the world. It also supplies the power called Life. What medics call a "stroke" indicates a weakness of nervous force in that part of the body affected. This proves that Life in the body is the result of this force.

But what is the nature of this force? Whence its source? It cannot come from the brain, for the brain is matter and cannot supply that force nor generate it. And science cannot solve that secret.

The world, in darkness, looks to science for Light, and the scientists are searching for the same things the layman is. Their nerves and brain give them no more knowledge of the mysteries of Life than these organs give to the layman. If you mention to a scientist what we say here, he will scorn it and can it hog-wash and hokum. He will advise you to disregard it. And with childish gullibility you will heed his advice. For you do no thinking of your own. You are not trained to think, but to have faith and believe what you are taught.

The universe and everything in life appear to every man according to the state of his brain and nervous system. That is the reason why no two people perceive the same universe. That accounts partly for the different opinions and conclusions that appear in the books and rule civilization. And he who opposes any of these things is a nut. Do not harken to or heed him, for if you do, you will go astray.

Chapter No. 9 – Magic Wires

"All our senses are represented in the central nervous system, but the terminals of the taste or palatine nerve tract from the tongue and the olfactory nerve tract from the nose, have not yet been found. They core within the temporal lobe of the brain, but the specific neurons associated with them are still unknown" (Yelena Saparina, in *Cybernetics within Us*).

In the previous chapter we sketched thru the human temple and located the Kingdom of God. We found it is centered in the brain and nervous system. As the brain would be useless without the nervous system, we must now consider these Magic Wires. Man knows almost nothing about his nervous system, and the medics are not much better off. And these magic wires fill the physical body so completely, that a pin cannot be pressed against the body anywhere without touching a nerve.

Man would be amazed if he could see in its entirety the nervous system of his body. It would present to the eye the same size, shape and form of the body itself.

That nervous system consists of what may be symbolically termed telephone wires that carry messages to and from the brain. And these wires are interlaced, interwoven, and interblended so completely with all parts of the body, that in our sight the nervous system and the physical body appear as one. We are gazing all the time at the Spiritual Man, the Lord from Heaven, but know it not.

The books, the schools, and medical science teach and believe that the nerves begin in the brain and terminate in various parts and organs of the body. if that were true, then from the brain would have to come the force that makes the body function, the heart to beat, and, in fact, the very Life of the body.

A great mystery is involved at this very point. We have never found it considered and explained in any of the books. It is unknown to medical science and also to the school of chiropractic.

The physical nerves do originate and begin in the brain. But we must go beyond the brain to discover the source of everything we want to know, and for which we are searching in this work to solve the magic and mystery that baffles science and the world as to the secret of Life.

The story we shall relate here will be scorned by the world, and science will attempt to discredit it by means of clever distinctions. But science admits that it cannot explain the mystery of Life, and dodges the question by asserting that what the world calls Life, in the case of man, is nothing more than the expression of a series of chemical changes. That is what Dr. Osler said, and he is regarded as the greatest physician America ever produced. We shall now present some facts relative to the work of Creation. All created formations that we see and know, are now found to be constituted of electro-magnetic energy, crystallized into what we consider by our known senses to be solid substance. This substance is now said to have originally evolved from the condensing clouds of ionized gases in the relative vacuum of space.

The atoms of this substance were produced by a force or power, the nature of which is not yet even faintly understood. And Man, the product of this creative action, is capable of thinking and striving to determine what he is, what life is, and what is his final goal. The nerves that begin in the brain as physical fibers, are the crystallized portion of the magical Silver Cord, mentioned in the Bible (Eccl.12:6), but ignored by science because it never stoops so low as to give credence to any statement in the bible.

This Silver Cord is an invisible radar beam that links with the Macrocosm the Microcosm which it has produced. After the Microcosm is created, the force from the Silver Cord, extending from the Empyreal Sea, penetrates the head (Golden Bowl) (Eccl. 12:6) at the soft spot called the Fonticulus Frontalis.

This special spot is kept saved by the Pope and the Catholic Priests, and a little cap is worn over it. We suspect they keep it shaved to make it easier for the Lord from Heaven to enter their body.

That's another secret relative to Magical Man unknown to the protestant pastors, and also to the medics and chiropractors. These doctors pay no particular attention to this important fontanel, mentioned in the Bible as "a door opened in heaven," indicating that the Ancient Magi knew all about this secret of Creation and the mystery of Life. Of the seven fontanels in the human skull, this one is much the larger, and remains open for a considerable time after birth. It presents a rhythmic pulsation that accords with the beating of the heart. And yet science does not realize the fact that much of the secret of Life is involved at this spot. This invisible Silver Cord, the existence of which is unknown to science is analogous to a radar beam that extends for miles into space, and along which air-planes may be guided accurately and safely.

The Silver Cord is connected with the germ cell that forms the embryo in the mother's uterus, and remains attached all thru life and until the death of the body. The basic cause of death is the separation of the Silver Cord from the human temple. Doctors have reported many instances of patients, undergoing operations, who leave their body during that time and look down on the unconscious shell.

In such cases, Spiritual Man is evulsed from the physical shell, and yet remains united to it by the Silver Cord, and by the means of which the Spiritual Man returns to the body and reactivates the shell, provided the Cord is not broken. The Silver Cord is capable of infinite extension. In sleep, we may, in our dreams, leave our body thru the "door opened in heaven," and fly miles away in a few seconds. And we return to the body as long as the Silver Cord remains intact. but when it breaks, somatic death results.

What is the character of Spiritual Man as he inhabits the body? That is another mystery unknown to science and the clergy. We find that answer in the ancient philosophy of Fire. It appears in the Bible in these words, "God is a consuming Fire" (Heb. 12:29 etc.).

The first religion of which we have any accurate account was that of Atlantis. This religion was the Philosophy of Fire, and it regarded Spiritual Man as the Divine Flame.

Universal electricity flows from the Empyreal Sea thru the Silver Cord, into the Brain, into the nerves, and out thru the body in the nervous system. That is the animating element. That is the power that moves muscles, arms, legs, body, and makes the heart, beat. All body functions can be reduced to electrical activity. The human temple is literally charged with electricity. Nervous force is electrical impulses flowing thru the nervous system, and electrical discharges crackle in the nerve cells.

Fate Magazine for September 1967 mentioned the case of a man named Brian Clements, of Harrow, England, whose body is so highly charged with electricity, that when he touches metal there is a faint bluish flash. When the Ego leaves the body at the moment of death, a faint bluish flash appears at the top of the head which can be seen by a clairvoyant. Brian Clements is quoted as saying, "I think the true reading for me would be nearer 10,000 volts, but I have no machine big enough to measure such a large amount" (p. 29). The body dies when Cosmic Electricity, the Silver Cord, fails to penetrate the brain and flow thru the nervous system. Why should it ever fail? Why do electric lights in your home fail? It's not the power that fails but the instrument in which the power operates,

This subject is covered more fully in our work titled *The Empyreal Sea.*

Chapter No. 10 – Magic Sensology

"Within the past century science has discovered a new world which it is just beginning to explore. But the evident vastness and richness are beyond either imagination or computation at this time (Guy Atherton, in *Strange Powers*, 1959).

Due to man's limited ability to receive and register relative knowledge with his five senses, there are vast states of creative action and production that lie beyond his reach. That is the world of the unknown.

In the acquisition of relative knowledge, man has made only limited use of his powers of reception and perception in the quest of observing and analyzing the exact nature of Force and Matter in their varying states. This is largely the fault of those by whom he is controlled, whose first task is to keep his knowledge limited and keep him in ignorance, thus making it easier to persuade him to swallow and believe the teaching of the institutions that rule civilization.

For instance, an intelligent man who thinks would never believe the fairy tale, that a God, way off in the sky, so loved the world, a tiny speck in space, that he gave his only begotten Son, that whosoever believeth in him should not perish, but have everlasting life (John 3:16). The Bible itself teaches that man does not perish, and is endowed with everlasting life (1 Cor. 15:51, 52 etc.).

In its recent discovery of a new world, science is surprised to find that space is not a vacuum as it had been thought to be. Instead of "nothingness' in space, science now asserts that out there in that invisible space all kinds of elements and substance exist.

Astronomers are able to determine that space is filled with gas, dust, and magnetic fields by measuring its absorption and effect on starlight. This gas and dust form solids and liquids, and these states are only varying degrees of one cosmic substance called universal electricity.

On this point we shall quote what Dr. David J. Calicchio, M.D., said: —

"Thru all the remarkable instances of the mystery of life, we see at all times one great force at work. The entire universe is moved by the positive and negative forces of electrical action. And all the operations of Nature in the Earth and its elements are carried on by the same power.

"Whether it be crystallizations or petrifactions, the growth of vegetation or its decomposition—motions and changes in the air and water—or the crumbling particles of the mountain rock—all the motions visible and invisible that transpire in the mineral and vegetable kingdoms, and in all their multifarious operations, are produced by electricity, which is the universal agent employed (by Creation) to keep up the harmony and order of the Universe" (Electronology, p. 39).

In the changes of solids to liquids and of liquids to gases, due to the limitation of man's Five Senses, science has had to resort to mathematics to become aware of the existence of the states of Matter which the Five Senses cannot register.

Science has discovered that Matter exists in states which the eye cannot see, of colors the eye cannot distinguish, of sounds the ear cannot hear, of odors the nose cannot detect, of flavors the tongue cannot taste, and, in general, of the existence of solids, liquids, gases and atomic particles which the Five Senses cannot record. In the process of acquiring knowledge of these various substances, science has learned that an exact law of mathematical sequences is operative in all phenomena.

The Ancient Magi knew that all manifestations of relativity are divided into multiples of Seven as a fundamental application of natural mathematical law, and that each division of Seven again has its Seven mathematical variations, and so on ad infinitism.

By deduction and analogy, the Ancient Magi also discovered that man possesses Seven Sense Organs, and determined the possible range of the function of the two extra senses, unknown to science.

When definite evidence of the existence of these two extra senses appears to science by accident or chance, physical scientists dismiss the subject by terming it Blind Instinct. That expounds nothing. It hides ignorance and indirectly admits the existence of sensory powers which scientists cannot analyze.

This is where the Superstitious Heathens of antiquity show us something. They located the centers of these two extra sense powers, learned how to resurrect and activate them, and also determined the approximate extent of their function. As physical man is a structural pattern of all Creation, we discover by deduction and analogy that he is not limited to Five Sense Powers, but possesses Seven.

Science denies the existence of these two extra sense powers. The last book of the Bible, an allegory which the Christian World cannot fathom, treats exclusively, in symbol and parable, of the Sixth and Seventh Sense powers, thus revealing how well the secret of these extra sense powers was known to the Ancient Magi. Certain occultists have discovered that with the Sixth Sense, the Pituitary gland in the brain, due to the chemistry of the seven minute organs of that sense-organ-group which are activated by vibrations equivalent to the speed of light, man is able to receive, translate and transit vibratory impulses that reverberate, apparently without diminishing force, for thousands of years, thru which man can register and repeat any previous set of vibrations sent out over the same instrument, or by voluntary control or adjustment, the vibrations sent out by others which we know as Memory in its many phases.

In its negative or receptive phases, the Pituitary gland, the Sixth Sense organ in the brain, picks up these vibrations and correspondingly activates the entire nerve system of the body, to give man knowledge in terms of repeating the impulses of the other Five Senses.

The Pineal gland in the brain, the Seventh Sense Organ and king of them all, permits direct contact with cosmic vibration in controlled concentrations, and may be regulated to duplicate the vibratory manifestations in Creation, according to cosmic law.

The Seventh Sense Organ picks up vibrations that are calculated mathematically to establish speeds of varying degrees, corresponding to the varying degrees of the speed of Light squared.

In its active, functional state, the Pineal uses the vibrations of the Pituitary to attract free atoms and reproduce the vibrations of any phenomenon composed of atoms. We must keep in mind the fact that man is a dual being, an astral entity inhabiting a material mechanism. He is seeking greater knowledge, but fails to apply what he already has. The knowledge is here for which man is searching, but the powers of civilization which control him, keep him in darkness so he will not discover it.

The esoteric teaching of the Bible deals with these secrets relative to man, king of the earth, in whose body the Spirit of God dwells and performs its work in the visible world. This is the mystery to which the gospel Jesus referred when he said:

"The Father that dwelleth in me (in all of us), he doeth the worked" (Jn. 14:10).

The esoteric know that the Ark of the Covenant, which is known to all ancient nations, is the symbol of man. Having no resting place for ages, it corresponds to man in his pilgrimage thru the wilderness of the world, where he is seeking pleasure and rest which Trust be sought within the Ark (the body). For only there can be found the Golden Pot of Manna (the mind). The tablet of the law corresponds to the seed atom of the dense body. Within the Hunan Ark is the Rod of Aaron (spinal column), with its thirty-three pairs of nerves (Masonry 330), awaiting fructification by the waters of regeneration.

The conservation of the Water of Life (seminal fluid) is absolutely necessary for the blooming of Aaron's Rod. By it alone can the Pia Mater of the Brain and spinal cord activate the Sixth and Seventh Sense powers of the brain. This will lift man from the sensual animal to the superhuman state.

This powerful creative force, when harnessed for the Kingdom of Heaven's sake, will kindle the tricolored Serpentine Fire of the propagative centers, which will ascend to the brain, and awaken to activity the two ductless glands, the pituitary and the pineal, which are symbolized by the two Cherubim with outstretched wings on the Ark of the Covenant. This stream of blue, yellow and red light, ascending from the lower part of the spine, branches at the pons into two parts; the yellow, the color of the Sun, blends with the blue, the color of the Ego, and forms one stream which enters the pineal gland, the mysterious Seventh Sense Organ.

The other stream, made up of yellow and red, the latter the color of the Holy Spirit, enters the pituitary gland, which represents the Sixth Sense Organ. Later the two streams blend and produce a third color which is indescribable, as are all spiritual colors. It has a scintillating, opalescent appearance, which expresses Life untrammeled.

This si the Holy Shekinah Glory which shone over the Mercy Seat of the Ark in the Holy of Holies; and shining over the head of the mystic, it is the means by which he is known to his brother mystic in the dark as well as in the light. He needs no watch-charm, no ring, or grip, and no written credentials.

When one rises to the degree of Regeneration, Aaron's Rod will have budded in his own Ark, the body. He will have earned the right to the Holy of Holies, to commune with his God between the wings of the kneeling Cherubim. And he will possess the sensory power of the Superman, for whom nothing is covered that shall not be revealed; and hid, that shall not be known (Mat. 10:26).

Chapter No. 11 – Magic Chambers

"In the frontal sinus between the eyes is the seat of the Intellectual Divinity in man. There, in a gaseous material, is the essence known as Mental Spirit. The Ancient Magi termed this the Lost City in the Sacred Desert, connected with the lower world by the Rainbow Bridge, or the Silver Cord. And it is to this point in himself, the Kingdom of God within, that man is striving to rise. ... If he would see the Sacred City in the Lotus Blossom, he must first open the Lotus within himself' (Manly Hall, *Initiates of the Flame*, 1922).

Not long ago science claimed the air was empty and void. Thousands of years ago the Ancient Magi taught that "The Essence of the Universe is in the Infinite Air in eternal movement which contains all in itself."

All animals and insects exhibit uncanny powers. Hornets and wasps have always known how to make paper. They were never taught the secret and needed no experience. Whence came their knowledge? Birds know which way to travel and when to go to avoid winter's icy blast. They know that snow will come at a certain time, and they must fly in a definite direction to a certain region to escape the fate of being frozen to death. Whence care their knowledge? Science has no logical answer for these questions. The best it can do is to claim it is "blind instinct." What is that?

Modern physics has studied phenomena in matter around us. That brand of physics died with the discovery of the electron. Physicists are now trying to rake the electron fit their materialism. They refuse to believe the electron belongs to another world, — the Spiritual World of the Ancient Magi.

The discovery of radio, radar and television are mechanized examples of the Spiritual Powers that operate as Cosmic

Intelligence in the conduct of birds and beasts which science calls "blind instinct." Why does man not possess these powers? The Ancient Magi taught that there is a Spiritual Realm in man. They said the Kingdom of God in within you (Lu. 17:21). That includes everything.

The Spiritual Realm in men is located in the brain and nervous system. We leave some of the darkness and find some Light when we learn that the Bible is the Book of Man, and refers to man in symbol and allegory and his journey through life. The Book With Seven Seals mentioned in Revelation (Chap. 5) is the human body, and the Seven Seals symbolize the Seven Gates (chakras, nerve centers) thru which the Golden Oil must flow to raise man's Consciousness to the psychic plane (Zech. 4:10-14).

The Seven Seals are mentioned in the Upanishads as Seven Chakras, and chakra means wheel. They are seven leading nerve ganglia linking the two chains of the vagus nerve system. In the very ancient Hindu scroll, which became the last book of the Bible and was written thousands of years before the world ever heard of the gospel Jesus, the Seven Sensorial Centers of the body were named in Hindu terminology as follows:

1.   Muladhara Chakra — At spinal base, between sexual organ and anus. It was called the Fish Gate or fundamental Lotus, and has four petals.

Each chakra was related to one of the cosmic elements. This one was symbolized by the earth, and its color is yellow. He who masters this chakra was said to have acquired knowledge of the past and future.

2. Svadhishthana Chakra — At the root of the procreative organ. It has control over the lower abdomen, kidneys, etc. It is the prostatic plexus, the ganglia at the base of the spinal canal, termed the coccygeal nerves that extend to the procreative glands.

The sciatic nerve, largest in the body, rises from these ganglia. This chakra has six petals, and its color is red. It symbol is water.

3.   Manipura Chakra — This is the solar plexus, or sun center, near the navel. Twelve nerve ganglia stem from it in different directions.

Each nerve branching from this center, forms a channel thru which the psycho-physical seed passes every 28 or 29 days. This chakra is the color of dark clouds, and has ten petals. Its symbol is fire.

4.   Anahata Charka — This is the cardiac plexus, formed by nerves of the cervical ganglia. Its color is a deep red. It has twelve petals, is the seat of Prana, and its symbol is air.

5.   Vishuddha Chakra — The pharyngeal plexus, at the base of the throat, below the larynx. It has sixteen petals, its color is white, and its symbol is ether.

We have now passed beyond the body and reached the head, the seat of the mysterious Sixth and Seventh Sense powers.

6.   Ajna Chakrar — The psycho-physical plexus of the spiritual chambers in the center of the forehead, where the two nostrils converge.

We now enter the field of the unknown, and science claims this field is empty, a vacuum, a realm of nothingness. The ancient scriptures are filled with references to a Spiritual World. Physical science holds that such a world is a myth, a figment of the imagination—that all is material substance and mechanical energy. The Ancient Magi regarded man as a miniature Universe. In that case, if there is a Spiritual World in the Universe, there must be the same in man. If that be true, his body must possess the essential organs by the means of which he is competent to contact the Spiritual World.

We might be lost in darkness had man not invented Radio, Radar and Television.

Man is a copyist and an imitator. He copies and imitates Creation's work. He can invent nothing that Creation has not produced. He simply selects, cuts, fits and arranges in a certain way the material Creation has furnished. By the use of his inventions, man now takes messages and pictures out of the air and presents them in his home. Had that magic been suggested to him before the time of his invention, he would have scorned the suggestion as the dream of a dunce.

By similar means, but on a far more perfect scale, Creation has provided in the human skull Five Chambers which bring man messages and pictures from anywhere on earth, the best illustration of that known to us being the case of Apollonius, as we have mentioned in another place.

These Chambers, the purpose and function of which are a mystery to science, were called the Five Stars of the Microcosm by the Ancient Magi, and were esoterically symbolized in ancient scriptures by various fives, such as the Five Golden Emerods, the Five Loaves, etc. (1 Sam. 6:4; Mat. 14:17).

The Secret Doctrine of the Ancient Magi stated that the Five Common Sense Powers of the body of conscious man are the exteriorized portion of the Five corresponding Spiritual Chambers in the human skull, which contact the world by means of the Nerve System.

These mysterious chambers are as follows:

1.   Frontal Sinus — A cavity in the frontal bone of the skull.

2.   Sphenoidal Sinus — A cavity in the sphenoid bone of the skull.

3.   Maxillary Sinus — Largest of the five, and in shape resembles a pyramid.

4.   Palatine Sinus — A cavity in the orbital process of the palatine bone.

5.   Ethmoidal Sinus — This chamber consists of several small cavities occupying the labyrinth of the ethmoid bone. In these cavities are situated the small, mysterious glands known to the Esoteric as the Intellectual Organs.

These Spiritual Chambers connect directly or indirectly with the nasal cavity, and receive the raw stream of air as it flows thru the nostrils, before any organ of the body has a chance to select and absorb anything from the Spiritual Essence of the Universe contained in the air, now known to be charged with everything that appears on the face of the earth. From the air everything comes, and to the air everything returns, as we have expounded in our great work titled *The Empyreal Sea*.

The Sinuses are lined with a very delicate mucous membrane, filled with nerves, and extending into them from the nostrils. To them rapidly spread all disorders that affect the air organs, such as cold, catarrh, influenza, pneumonia, etc. They receive with no protection the full force of all poisonous gases and acids in the air. In this world of polluted air it's not surprising that the Sixth Sense Power in man is dormant.

Man would be shocked if he knew how seriously his powers of perception are injured by the polluted air that causes the "simple cold." Right there, as a baby, is where he begins to lose some of the power that informs him of all he knows. There is much in the world unknown to man because he lacks the power to perceive it. If his power of perception were increased a hundredfold, his knowledge of everything would be correspondingly increased. Such a man would stand with his feet upon the earth and his head among the stars. In certain books about Egypt appears a picture of Seti, ruler of Egypt 3300 years ago, with a Serpent at his forehead, representing the activation of the Ajna Chakra in the Spiritual Chambers by the Divine Fire contained in the air, and the Serpentine Fire of the Muladhara Chakra at the spinal base.

This chakra has two petals, and when affected by the dual fires mentioned, the petals bend down and out, forming the Winged Globe of the Egyptian Magi. Its principle is rental (Mamas), and its color is glittering white. This is called the All-Seeing Eye in the Bible (Mat. 6:22, etc.). It is indicated in ancient scriptures by a Jewel, and in Egyptian symbolism by a globe-crowned Serpent, or Winged Globe, for which reason Egypt was called the "Land of the Winged Globe."

In our work titled *"Awaken The World Within"* appears a strange picture, representing the dual Creative Principles, consisting of a body with two heads, a man's and a woman's, standing on *the Great Red Dragon* mentioned in the Bible (Rev. 12:1-6), from whose mouth a stream of Serpentine Fire issues. This symbolizes the Creative Essence of the Human Temple. Around the body appears symbols of the Seven Chakras. This picture is carved on stone monuments said to be ten thousand years old.

This vital center, tensed the Trikona by the Hindu Magi, was said to be the seat of Eternal Knowledge. It is exceedingly sensitive and, when not injured or practically ruined by polluted air or other harmful agencies, it manifests a high degree of Intelligence that makes man para-natural, with strong psychic powers, spiritual vision — vision of things and events not seen with physical eyes, as in the case of Apollonius. The Pituitary, the organ of the Sixth Sense, situated near this vital center, is the Master Gland of propagation. As woman is the productive agency, the Pituitary is more active in her brain on that account. This augments her consciousness and makes her more psychic than man, as a rule.

7.   Shasrare Chakra — Situated in the crown of the head, and the abode of Siva. The Catholic Priests keep this spot shaved and wear a little cap over the shaved spot.

This is the thousand-petalled lotus of the brain, and usually represented directly above the head in Hindu symbolism. What the Ancient Magi allegorically termed "the marriage of the Lamb," was the activation of the Pineal (male) by the Pituitary (female) as a result of a definite stimulation by the Golden Oil (seminal essence) that is raised up from the procreative centers at the spinal base, the point of the Muladhara Chakra (Rev. 19:7-9). At this point the Bible says, "And if Christ (Golden Oil, Seminal Essence) be not raised, your faith is vain; ye are yet in your sins" (of fornication) (1 Cor. 15:17).

The Bible refers to this again in these words:

"There is a sin unto death (Fornication). ... Whosoever is born of Cod (spiritual generation) doth not commit sin; for his SEED remaineth in him and he cannot sin. ... For in the day that thou eatest thereof (fornicate) thou shalt surely die" (by degrees) (Gen. 2:17; 1 John 3:9; 5:10).

The student will begin to understand the biblical allegories when he banishes religion from his mind and realizes that the Bible is the Book of Man.

The Seventh Sense Power, the marriage of the Lamb, rising from the activation of the Sahasrara Chakra and conferring on man the power of Seer-ship, was the Magical Field of the Ancient Magi. The Bible says:

'And when he had opened the seventh seal (chakra that affects the Pineal), there was SILENCE in heaven (brain) about the space of half an hour' (Rev. 8:1).

Then a little later the Bible speaks again in these words:

"He had in his hand a little book open; and he put his right foot upon the sea, and his left foot upon the earth, and cried with a loud voice, as when a lion roareth; and when he had cried, Seven Thunders uttered their voices. And when the Seven Thunders had uttered their voices, I was about to write; and I heard a voice from heaven (the kingdom of God within) saying unto me, Seal up those things which the Seven Thunders uttered, and write then not" (for that is secret magic teaching) (Rev. 10:2-4).

This magic is involved in Arcanum XIV of the ancient Tarot, symbolizing the Genie of the Sun holding a golden urn in one hand and a silver urn in the other, and pouring from the one to the other the precious Fluid of Life (Seminal Essence). Now this Genie of the Sun is the real I AM, or the Ego of the human race, having its seat in the Tiphareth, the sixth Sephirah. He is shown adapting and modifying the personal stream of Psychic Energy in the action and reaction of the conscious and subconscious aspects of human personality.

This is the Forbidden Field to which Paul (Apollonius) referred when he said:

"And I knew such a man, how that he was caught up into paradise, and heard unspeakable words (as symbolized in the third degree of Freemasonry), which it is not lawful for a man to utter" (2 Cor. 12:3,4).

Again the Bible speaks and says: "And the seventh angel poured out his vial into the air; and there came a great voice from the temple of heaven, from the throne (brain), saying HE IS BORN" (Rev. 16:17).

Who was born? Ask some Mason who is a member of the Blue Lodge of Freemasonry. He should know, for he went thru the ritual in the Third Degree. But he does not know because the real secret was not expounded to him. Perhaps the Master of Ceremonies did not know the deep secret involved.

HE IS BORN signified the death of degenerate ran of Five Sense powers and the birth of Regenerate man of Seven Sense Powers, the Sage and Seer, as indicated in our work titled *"AWAKEN THE WORLD WITHIN."* What the Ancient Magi wrote about this Forbidden Field was always heavily veiled in symbol and parable and was interpreted to the Neophyte in Initiation.

Neither would it be proper for us to analyze the secret of this Forbidden Field in any terms but the most general. Only a few can comprehend what we say, and fewer still will believe it.

The mysterious Pineal gland in the brain, the function of which science knows nothing, is the organ of memory, of expectation and anticipation, of spiritual vision, and of Seer ship. It never forgets, and contains all the wisdom of past ages. Because this gland is dormant or semi-dormant, some people have poor memory, some have little, others have almost none. If this organ were in full function, a man's memory would extend back, thru his childhood days, and on back before he was born, into his antecedent incarnation. The less active the Pituitary and Pineal, the weaker the memory and consciousness. Some increase in the activity of these glands may be produced by deep concentration of thought.

Certain dreams result from the action of these glands. Due to deep concentration of thought, some people may get a glimpse of their days in a prior incarnation and not understand them. Certain knowledge may come to them in dreams, and they may see future events that will come to pass.

Look not to physical science for any data in this Forbidden Field, for science claims it is all hog-wash and hokum.

Chapter No. 12 – The Magician

"Man is a center of specific activities. He appears as distinct from the inanimate world. ... Personality extends beyond the physical organism.... It diffuses thru space in a positive way. Man's psychological frontiers in space and time are obviously suppositions. ... In telepathic phenomena, he instantaneously sends out a sort of emanation, which joins a faraway relative or friend. He thus expands to great distances. He may cross oceans and continents in a time too short to be estimated" (Dr. Alexis Carrel, in *Man The Unknown*).

The world should know that all orthodox medics are materialists, evolutionists, and atheists. Their books and the teaching of their schools do not recognize anything beyond the limit of the material world. It was Carrel's unorthodox in this respect that caused him to be ostracized by the medical fraternity and lose its favor and respect. Arcanum No. 1 of the ancient Tarot was titled The Magician. In fact, the various commentators called it Magus, Magician and Juggler. It presented the picture of a youthful figure, clad in the robe of a Magician. Above the head hovered a symbol of the Life Link, mentioned in the Bible as the Silver Cord (Eccl. 12:6). It links together physical man and spiritual man as expounded in our work titled "*The Flare Divine.*" This symbol indicated the Macrocosmic character of the Magician. It signified that he embodied the Creative Principle and personified the tetradic qualities of the living organism known as Consciousness, Mind, Intelligence, and Vitality.

About his waist was a Serpent Cincture, the serpent appearing to swallow its tail, forming a Circle, the ancient symbol of Eternity. In his left hand, pointing upward, was the Magic Wand, the serpent-wound staff of Hermes, symbol of the Creative Power, Polarity—without which there could be no creation. His right hand pointed downward toward the earth, indicative of the ancient exiom, "As above, so below," the physical world being a reflection of the Spiritual World.

Before him stands a square table, signifying the four hypothetical corners of the world. On the table are scattered four symbols which represent the Four Universal Elements which constitute the physical world.

This brings before us that point around which much mystery is woven. It would take a large book to examine and expound it all. This involves the strange symbol called the Sphinx. It involves the Lost Word of Freemasonry. It involves the secret of the Four Letters of the Ineffable Name, J H V H.

It is interesting to observe how the biblical makers brought this mystery into action. We quote:

"And God spake unto Moses, and said unto him, I am the Lord: And I appeared unto Abraham, unto Isaac, and unto Jacob, by the name of God Al-mighty (El Shaddai), but by my name JE HO VA H was I not known to them" (ex. 6:2,3). This fourfold primal basis of Creation appears on each level of integration in a different guise, and is discussed in detail in our work titled *"Cosmic Creation."*

The exoteric don't know that these Four Cosmic Symbols appear in a deck of common playing-cards, and are called Spades, Clubs, Hearts and Diamonds. By the ancients they were called Wands, Cups, Coins and Swords. The two colors represent Polarity.

This brings us to the real Magician in the flesh. He was a man of history, and his body was so well developed and conditioned, that he presented evidence of the existence of Eternal Knowledge.

This exceptional man lived in the First Century of this era. The news of his remarkable powers of perception went out to the world in which he lived. That's why it attracted the attention of the Church Fathers when they were searching the records in the

Fourth Century, looking for a great character to play the role of their Jesus of the gospels.

This gospel Jesus was a renowned Pythagorean philosopher. He revealed his powers of Spiritual Vision in an amazing manner while preaching in Ephesus at the time when the Roman Emperor, Domitian, was assassinated. And, although many miles away, he actually saw the deadly deed done by the power of his television mechanism, situated in the sinuses of his skull.

We would not be able to understand this mystery had man not invented the television mechanism, which brings into our home messages and pictures from all over the world. How many more mysteries are there in the Universe unknown to us because we have no knowledge of them and no means to acquire it?

When the vision flashed in this man's television mechanism, he was surprised by what he saw. At first he lowered his voice as if terrified by the sight. Then, with less than his usual vigor of speech, he continued to Preach as if, between statements, he got a glimpse of something far away.

Finally, he lapsed into silence, as if he had been interrupted in his talk. And then, staring straight down, he advanced a few steps in an involuntary manner, and shouted in a loud voice, "Courage, Stephan us, smite the tyrant." And Stephanus did smite him.

According to history, this was the greatest man of the First Century of this era. The Christian Fathers considered him so great that they made him the Jesus of the gospels, the Paul of the Epistles, and the John of Revelation. We have told his story in our work titled *"Mystery Man Of The Bible."*

Read the story of Apollonius of Teaneus. In his book, *"Mystic Rebels,* Prof. Harry C. Schnur said:

"Pythagorean thought filtered and purified the diverse rites and cults that, from time to time, became fashionable, and great reformers synthesized all these elements into a whole of remarkable wisdom, purity and lofty ethical teaching. The greatest of these reformers of the ancient faith was Apollonius" (p. 14).

Apollonius acted like he saw with his own eyes the shocking event when Stephanus killed Domitian. After a short pause, he said to his congregation, "Rejoice, my friends, for the tyrant dies this day. Yea, at the moment in which I was silent, he paid with his life for his crimes." This fact was soon confirmed by a messenger from Rome, who brought the tidings. The Emperor was stabbed to death in his bedroom on September 18, 96 A.D., by a freeman of Clemens named Stepnanus. And Apollonius, miles away, actually saw the deed done. We could not understand this had man not copied the work of Creation in his invention of the television mechanism. Think what it would mean if we all had the television mechanism in our head in operation so we could get visions and messages like that.

It's reasonable to assume that the body does not have to die to resurrect and activate Spiritual Man's super consciousness. A somewhat similar state prevails when the body is unconscious in sleep, and the five senses are inactive. Maybe this is the dreaming stage. While much that happens is too strange to be understood, nothing is too strange to happen. And words were invented to deal only with the effects which we see and not with the cause which produces the effects. The effects are the surface aspect of what happens, with no knowledge of the hidden cause. What happens is known to our five senses by the visible sign of the operation on an invisible, dynamic force that is a harmony in time as well as in space.

Rents said: *"The vice of the Soul is ignorance, and the virtue of the Soul is knowledge."*

Dr. Rhys David wrote: *"It is not by chance that the foundation of the higher life, the gate to the heaven that is to be reached on earth, is not placed in emotion, nor in feeling, but in knowledge, in victory over delusion and ignorance."*

Slumber blacks out the five senses of the body which inform man of the external world, and usually lead him astray. The black-out releases Spiritual Man from the shackles of the body, and permits the attunement of the mind with Eternal Knowledge. Wise men consider ignorance as mankind's great curse. That ignorance is the design of the false teaching man receives from childhood up. He must be kept in ignorance as to the facts of Creation so he will support the fraudulent institutions which control our grand civilization.

If Eternal Knowledge did not exist, it could not be perceived by man at any time, whether awake or asleep. And why should it be beyond our reach when awake, and come to us when the body is unconscious in sleep? There are several reasons for that.

Why should any knowledge exist if it were not to be perceived by man and used for his benefit? Why should any knowledge man may need not be available to him at all times? To these questions we have a partial answer. Religion thrives on ignorance, and is based on faith and superstition.

These qualities make man a stupid slave of the priesthood. Accordingly, in the 4th, 5th, and 6th centuries the Mother Church sought to improve conditions for the priesthood by destroying knowledge and reducing man to the lowest level of ignorance and superstition. And to preserve this condition, for a thousand years all education was banned in the Roman Empire, and even kings and rulers of nations could not read nor write. And to think that this Church still stands, and is supported by millions of religious fanatics, who are taught to believe that their Jesus has washed them of their sins in his own blood. (Rev. 1:5).

They should remember the biblical statement that man reaps as he sows (Gal. 6:7); for that is the inexorable law of Creation, and no one can escape it regardless of what the Church teaches about Jesus and salvation.

It has been only within the last two centuries that the Christian World, due to the declining power of the Church, has begun to emerge from the Dark Ages which covered more than a thousand years. And already, in that comparatively short time, so much lost knowledge has been recovered that a new world is looming up before us. The evidence indicates that within the coming century, hidden knowledge of the mysteries of Creation may be revealed that will startle the world.

After his birth, man is on his own insofar as cooperating with the immutable laws of Creation are concerned. This is where Free Will enters. At any point, in any age of man, he can be free. There is nothing holding him at any level except the things he himself has created. He is liberated from all fixed laws that rule Cosmic Consciousness by the endowment of Free Will; and how he may use it, whether positively or negatively, measures his individual degree of progression or retrogression.

We are too prone to accept as basic facts what is commonly taught in schools, in universities, in religion and in medicine. There is no sound reason why we should refuse to consider thoughts that are different from those regularly taught.

We must always remember and never forget that back of all teaching are design, purpose, plan. And those who rule the teaching expect to profit from the effect which the teaching produces on the mind of those who are taught.

Chapter No. 13 – Magic Light

"Oh Mysteries most truly holy. Oh pure Light. When the torch of the Dadoukos gleams, Heaven and the Deity are revealed to my eyes. I am initiated and become holy" (Albert Pike, *Morals & Dogma*, p. 522). LIGHT is a symbol of Knowledge. Plutarch compared Isis to Knowledge and Typhon to Ignorance, obscuring the Light of the sacred doctrine whose Flame Lights the Ego of the Initiate. He held that no gift of the gods was so precious as the Knowledge of Life.

Clements of Alexandria declared that the basic purpose of initiation in the Ancient Mysteries was to emancipate man from his passions, and to liberate his mind from the control of the senses. Then man was freed from darkness and his mind was illuminated by Divine Knowledge. And such man knew his eternal home was among the Stars. It is painful for us to realize and admit that our boasted civilization, when broadly considered, is composed of two general classes, to-wit, (1) the fraudulent institutions which control civilization, and (2) the gullible masses who are schooled to serve and support them.

The success of the former depends on the ignorance and darkness (John 3:9). And to deceive the masses it strives by every hook and cook to rake the masses believe that their good and welfare are at heart. That makes it expedient for schools and universities to be operated and controlled by these fraudulent institutions. And the job is so fully and carefully performed, that it's almost impossible to make the hood-winked, blind, credulous, gullible, stupid, thinkless, mind-controlled, brainwashed masses believe they are misled, miseducated, duped, deceived, oppressed, suppressed, and systematically kept in ignorance and darkness.

These fraudulent institutions have little interest in such serious matters as Cosmic Consciousness and Eternal

Knowledge, and no helpful teaching on these subjects is allowed in the schools, nor put in the books. That is the reason why the world in general knows so little about the principles called Cosmic Consciousness and Eternal Knowledge. Even professional writers and renowned authors of books are so confused in this field that they have no clear conception of these principles.

When we consult the dictionary as to these principles, this is what we find:

Consciousness: The knowledge of sensations and mental operations, or of what passes in one's own mind; the state of being conscious. Knowledge: A clear and certain perception of that which exists, or of truth and fact; the perception of that connection and agreement, or disagreement and repugnance of our ideas. These dictionary definitions are the essence of that which is taught in schools and books relative to the broad, life-controlling principles that make a man a driveller or a master, a slave or a sage.

We have noticed the various conditions involved which regulate and govern man's state of consciousness and knowledge. The main one is what man is taught from childhood up. And not many persons ever change their mind from that which was taught them when they were children.

That teaching is carefully designed, being the result of years of experience, and is formulated to fix man's mind for the regular groove in which it shall journey thru life and support the fraudulent institutions which rule civilization, consisting of religion, medicine, banking, commercialism, industrialism, etc.

Man's level of intelligence is what his Consciousness is. If that be true, it is essential, indispensable, and imperative that we strive to determine what Consciousness is; whence its source, and what's its nature.

We are told that all created formations, iron atoms up, are alive; and all living things are endowed by Creation with a state of intelligence called Cosmic Consciousness. They all know their appointed work, know how to perform it, and are able to do it. The flower, vine and tree, the bug, bird and beast, all possess a certain degree of Consciousness, and by that power are ruled and guided thru life.

This is another aspect of Creation that is a mystery to science. Scientists call this mysterious state Blind Instinct, but know not what it actually is. Giving meaningless names to the unknown, and pushing it back in a corner solves no problems. But that is the common course science takes and a stupid world believes science knows. The lowest known state of Cosmic Consciousness appears in atoms. It progressively increases in ratio with the degree of development of the living formation, reaching its highest point in man, who is said in the Bible to be the Lord of the whole earth (Zech. 4:14).

And here we meet another peculiar condition to which science gives little or no attention. Man is endowed with specialized power that enables him to stand with his feet on the Earth and his head in the Empyrean. And this exalted state, called Free Will, is for man alone, and designed to lift him up to the Angelic Plane. But it has been the basic cause of sinking him into the mire of degeneration. And science does not realize it. The more knowledge we gain in every respect, the more we learn how little we know of the mysteries of Creation. There's a ring-pass-not that we cannot penetrate regardless of the direction we take.

The great work of Creation occurs in the invisible realm, and it's impossible for us to know the finality of even the simplest object. Hence, the datum of the ultimate origin and nature of Consciousness seems to lie beyond the scope of our perception. But he cannot advance who folds up and seeks no farther than the known, and believes that the commonly unknown cannot be fathomed. New knowledge and new discoveries keep coming up before us, and that should encourage us to keep on searching.

There is a serious obstacle in our path. New knowledge and new discoveries that shatter fixed beliefs and pet opinions are unwelcome. Even scientists, when faced with unorthodox claims, back away, attack him who makes them, and even deny the evidence of their own findings to hide their ignorance that is exposed by new knowledge and new discoveries. They are as unwilling today to investigate new claims as they were in the Middle Ages. In his writing on this subject, one author said: "Cosmic Consciousness is as far superior to ordinary Consciousness as the latter is superior to the Blind Instinct of the lower animals."

He who proffers such postulate as his major premise, reveals thereby his own ignorance of both Cosmic Consciousness and Blind Instinct. We'll notice both terms and seek to show that they refer to the same principle. Cosmic Consciousness is the term invented that means the power which guides, directs, and controls all of the involuntary functions of the Human Temple, the highest and greatest organization ever produced by Creation. And those functions never go wrong nor astray, regardless of the false claims of the medics that they do. That same power guides, directs, and controls the flowers of the field and the beasts of the forest. This means that all living creatures below men correspond in all their habits to the laws of Creation. That power inheres in and rises from the atom.

The atom has now been discovered to be a miniature solar system, with stars, satellites, and planets, on all of which are engraved the events extending from the present back to the infinite past. This means that in the realm of atoms the element of Time does not exist. The status of Consciousness becomes more comprehensible as we learn that common human

Consciousness is but one phase thereof, and that higher and lower phases exist. In itself, a state of Consciousness is neither high nor low. It becomes subject to classification in comparison with other states. What is high in one instance may be low in another.

Some examples will serve to show various states of Consciousness. Rudolph Steiner presented in his book titled *Cosmic Memory,* the case of bees and ants and their work. But he was unable to describe definitely in words what he had in his mind. Steiner showed that the amazing collaboration of various classes of in-sects — males, females, and workers — proceeds in a systematic fashion, ruled by infinite Consciousness that knows the end from the beginning. This mystic power ruling the activity of insects is what a misguided science calls Blind Instinct.

To follow that system of science means to be led by the blind; and when the blind leadeth the blind, they all fall into the ditch (Mat. 15:14). And that is precisely and definitely the state in which the world of science flounders at this very time. And the gullible masses think they are traveling the right road when they follow that science. The distribution of the various tasks among the several categories of insects, and their ability and intelligence to perform them according to the laws of creation, is a manifestation of that supreme state of Cosmic Consciousness, called Blind Instinct by science.

What occurs in the work of bees and ants is as much the result of a definite state of Consciousness as is the work of men in his world.

Man's systems of religion, medicine, commercialism, industrialism, art and science are the products of his Consciousness, and they indicate the state thereof. And the condition of confusion prevailing in man's world indicates a state of Consciousness that is extremely low. If man's Consciousness operated on a higher level, his artificial world called Civilization, his religion and all of the isms and ologies that are crushing the gullible masses to the earth, would be quickly changed to a more natural and far better condition.

The state of Consciousness at the base of the bee-hive and ant-hill, a mystery to physical science and stupidly called Blind Instinct, rules the bugs and birds. And so they live in harmony with the laws of Creation without having been taught anything. And they have no sickness, no doctors, no drugs, no hospitals, and are subject to the same laws which govern man.

That divine, supreme, unconditioned state of Consciousness flows un-modified from the cosmic source—from God the fanatical religionist would say. And he had rather live in darkness than to risk the result of an investigation of his God, and who declares with great firmness that only his God can grow a tree.

The great Sir Isaac Newton, profoundly religious and living in the latter days of the Dark Ages, believed he could find that God. At the conclusion of his searching he was shocked to find that we inhabit an automatic Universe in which heat, soil, water and air produce the entire vegetable kingdom, and do it without assistance from any God.

These are the Four Sacred Elements of the Ancient Magi which are enveloped in great mystery. They are symbolized by the Sphinx, signified by Arcanum IV of the Tarot as The Emperor, cited in the Bible as the strange letters J H V H, mentioned in the New Testament as "The Word made flesh," and that mysterious Lost Word of Freemasonry (Ex. 6:3; John 1:14). All of this is covered in our great work titled *"The Hidden Creator."* For we are here at the threshold of the great mystery of Creation. This is the main story concealed in the Zodiac, the four fixed signs of which symbolize (1) Fire (Leo, Lion), (2) Air (Scorpio, Eagle), (3) Water (Aquarius, Man), (4) and Earth (Taurus, Bull). Without these Four Universal

Elements, the Christian God would be helpless; and with them, he is useless, as Newton found.

Newton discovered the great principles of Creation, but was scared to elaborate on them because of the ruthless power of the Mother Church in his day and time, as it dealt death to those who did not stay in line.

Newton found that the principles of Creation consist of Polarity, Electro-magnetism, Heat, Cold, Expansion and Contraction, acting on atoms, causing them to perform their work which produces the infinite formations, according to the archetypal patterns that have no beginning, as expounded in our work titled *"Pre-existence Of Man."*

And the same orderly work of bees and ants, which has been in operation since they first appeared on earth, will continue without change for millions of years in the future, just as at present. There will be no "progress" as so-called progress is another illusion that deceives men. For Creation's work is perfect and cannot be improved by stupid man.

The processes of Creation never change because they are perfect. And the future hides no mysteries from those who learn the laws of Creation. In fact, the future, under the law, is NOW. Time is another illusion.

The circle, not a straight line, is the symbol of Eternity. Everything is eternal. There is changing but no ending. The Apostle Paul knew that, and he said, *"Behold, I show you a mystery: We shall not all sleep (in death), but we shall be changed, in a moment, in the twinkling of an eye"* (1 Cor. 15:51, 52).

Knowledge and Consciousness are eternal. They do not begin and end. Everything is now that has been or will ever be: The Bible teaches that: *"The thing that hath been, is that which shall be (again); and that which is done (now) is that which shall (always) be done; and there's no new thing under the sun"* (Eccl.

1:9). Man is the highest organized entity known. Being endowed with Free Will, he naturally exercises a prerogative not possessed by bees, birds and beasts. This superior endowment is for man's benefit, to exalt him to the angelic plane, high above the level of the animal kingdom. But the leaders and controllers of Civilization are careful to see that man is not aware of the purpose of that endowment.

And so man is taught to employ that endowment to sink him in the mire of degeneration and create a world of bad health that yields amazing profits for those who make it a business to live on the miseries of man. If properly used, that endowment would enable man to build up and express powers of a so-called superman. He would be the god designed at his creation. His world would be a paradise as it was intended to be, and there would be no priests, preachers, physicians, drugs, hospitals, insane asylums, etc. But that glorious estate is not wanted by the powers that rule civilization, and suitable measures have been taken to prevent it from coming to pass. To determine the power of Creation that rules and guides the Animal Kingdom, one cannot confine oneself to the physical world, where insects inhabit physical bodies. The power and its source must be sought beyond the physical realm.

This means of course that we must reject the misleading opinion of physical science, that "the world is composed of blind and unknown forces" (Dr. Alexis Carrel, in *Man the Unknown*, p. 16). It's no wonder that science is lost in darkness. We must not be deceived by the modified state of Consciousness exhibited by man. For that state has been conditioned and distorted by his prerogative.

The state called Blind Instinct which rules bees and ants, is not conditioned nor modified, and must be determined and sought in the Supersensible World. If man ascended to that world, he'd greet the "bee and ant spirit spirit" in a state of unmodified Cosmic Consciousness. The Seer and Clairvoyant can actually do that. This was one of the highly guarded secrets of Creation that was revealed to the Neophyte in the ritual of Initiation in the Ancient Mysteries five thousand years ago.

In the orderly work of bees and ants, we witness the conduct of entities that are ruled and guided exclusively by Cosmic Consciousness. That's the primeval state of Cosmic Consciousness called Blind Instinct by physical science. Ancient tradition indicates that it was this state of Consciousness that ruled and guided man when he lived a thousand years.

We are informed that ancient man's consciousness embraced a complete history of his entire existence. That was the condition way back in the early days, before man's evil conduct had caused such serious degeneration of his organism, even to the extent of rendering dormant in his body, more than a hundred organs that were designed by Creation to perform certain functions. These organs, now useless or partly so, are cited by science to show that man is the result of evolution. That theory is advanced to explain why his body has no use now for various organs that were needed and useful when man was in the ape stage.

When the people follow a science that dumb, it is understood why man believes the foolish fanaticism and fetishism that fill his mind. In rare cases some of these organs still perform faint functions in some people, and they do dimly recollect weak impressions of fragments of their previous life. Or they may be clairvoyants, or present other mental qualities that are an enigma to science.

These rare states serve to show that the ordinary consciousness of man is only a particular instance of consciousness, and that mysticism is a projection of Eternal Knowledge into our common condition of consciousness. And those who experience such states had better keep silent about it, or they may be viewed with suspicion. In this civilization but a few men know that they are oppressed, suppressed, misled, miseducated, deceived, kept in darkness, live only on the surface, and are ignorant and unconscious of what lies in their own depths—in the billions of solar systems of the atoms of their body and brain, on which are recorded the events of their being from the present back to eternity.

Since man possesses the power to rise above the state of Cosmic Consciousness that rules the bugs, birds and beasts, and possesses an awareness of his differences and characteristics, science has asked: What is Man? Once having gratified the cravings and demands of the beastilic phase of his nature, some men seek for the gratification of the angelic aspect of their being. Such higher-minded men encounter undesirable conditions on every side, as this line of higher living compels the rejection of the pleasures which the body craves because it has been bent in that direction by man's evil conduct.

This condition provides the place where religion and medicine move in, and grow rich and powerful by teaching the gullible passes that people may go right on yielding to the cravings of their body, and religion and medicine will remedy the evils that result from the pleasurable indulgences that the body craves, due largely to man's wrongful habits and the corruptible influence of civilization.

It's a grand scheme for the promoters, but it fails in practice and the masses do the suffering. Under the law, people must pay the penalty of their evil deeds and reap as they sow, regardless of religion and medicine. Side by side with the concept of hidden knowledge, there runs thru the whole history of human thought the idea of Superman. The dumb masses live with the idea of Superman. The fact is concealed from them that man is a miniature universe, having within himself everything known from mineral to vegetable, from animal to humanal, from Soul to Sun.

Prof. Hotema   The Magic World   Chapter No. 13

Man is not separated from Superman by time but by condition and ignorance. Man's mind is conditioned and closed by false teaching that prevents the entry into his mind of the higher knowledge which transforms Man to Superman. In our corruptible civilization of organized fraud, Superman is not wanted and is banished. He is dangerous. If he should happen to appear he would be summarily silenced and liquidated as the gospel Jesus was, 'for the good of the people.'

That factor in the story of Jesus is never noticed. The Bible says:

"Then gathered the chief priests and the Pharisees a council, and said, What do we? For this man doeth many miracles. If we let him thus alone, all men will believe on him; and the Romans shall come and take away both our place and our nation. And one of them, named Caiaphas, being the high priest that same year, said unto them, Ye know nothing at all, nor consider that it is expedient for us, that one man should die for the people, and that the whole nation perish not. And thus spake he not for himself: but being high priest that year, he prophesied (decreed) that Jesus should die for that nation" (John 11:47-51).

In Anthon's Classical Dictionary, we read:

"The only evil spirit which had an agency in the oracular responses of antiquity, was that spirit of crafty imposture which always finds so congenial a home among the artful and cunning priesthood."

It was that same priesthood who interpolated this statement in the Bible:

"If ye will obey my voice indeed, and keep my covenant, then ye shall be a peculiar treasure unto me above all people; for all the earth is mine and ye shall be unto me a Kingdom of Priests, and an holy nation." (Exod. 19:5,6).

In regard to 'the artful and cunning priesthood,' Dr. Wm. McCarthy wrote:

"The priesthood originated with, and developed under, the worship of mythical gods, so declared by all the world; hence, priest craft is built solely upon falsehood, and the motive controlling its origin and development was, and always has been, selfish and mercenary; its guiding star is gain and greed." (*Bible, Church & God*, p. 47).

And that's the character of the group of men who made gods of ancient symbols which represent the various powers and agencies of Creation. And the dumb masses still follow them.

Chapter No. 14 – Magic Attraction

'In the religions of almost all people, traces of sex and love cults can be found. In Armenia, Lydia, Persia, and Scythia the people worshipped Anaitis, to whom was consecrated young virgins and who prostituted themselves in her honor." (*Nagica Sexualis,* by Dr. Ernie Laurent & Prof. Paul Nagour,1968, p. 262).

The rare fragments of ancient history that have come down to us, disclose some amazing accounts of the habits and customs of ancient people, and especially in relation to religion and sexualism. It's not surprising that the first allegory in the Bible deals with that subject as the eating of the Forbidden Fruit.

In the book from which was excerpted the Quotation in the above heading, it is said: "If there is one prevalent superstition today, it would clearly be that sex is dirty and evil.'

That is the low, degraded condition of the procreative function of the human body that has resulted from man's evil work in abusing and mistreating the great process of the body, designed by Creation to carry on and perpetuate its work.

In the book above mentioned appears this statement:

"Creative nature has placed the highest pleasure in the union of the two sexes; and it is on this attraction, stretching from humanity to the animal kingdom, that there rests the certainty of eternal victory of life over death."

Propagation. is not a victory of life over death, it is the cosmic process of created objects to carry on the work originated by Creation. It's a remarkable factor that all created objects are endued with power to propagate, from the lowest weed up to man. And like the function of eating to sustain the body, the function of producing new bodies has been debased and degraded to the very bottom of the pit.

Sex has played an extremely important role in ancient religions. In India the God of Love and the symbol of sex is Kamadeva, who sprang forth fully armed from the flaming heart of Brahma. He has many names; god of lust, exciter of the spirit, of madness, the inflamer, the disturber of pious rest, etc. Krishna, whose erotic deeds are described in song in the Prem Sagur, is also the God of Love of the Hindus. But Siva is the god to whom most of the shrines are dedicated, the favorite symbol of the Siva cult being the lingam.

This replica of the male progenitive organ appears in great abundance at Cambodia, where every year at the celebration of the arrival of spring, a huge hollow lingam is led about in a procession thru the streets. The yogis wear the lingam around their necks and always offer it as the first fruits of all their feasts.

The masculine member is regarded by all the people of ancient days as the symbol of universal fructification. Its cult has grown to one of the most popular myths of India

The legends of India assert that the God Siva lives upon the Mountain of Gold, Kailasa, on which is a beautiful table, decorated with the most costly of stones. In the center of the table is a lotus flower, and in the center of the flower there is a triangle, the origin and source of all things. From this triangle there Proceeds a lingam, the eternal god, who lives in this residence.

Even now, after three thousand years, in spite of the Puritanism of England, the Hindus still worship these geometrical symbols of the lingam and the yoni. The lingam appears everywhere — in streets, roads, byways, public squares, fields, etc. The religious ceremonies are always impregnated with these same erotic tendencies. In Benares, the holy city of the Hindus, when the sun rises it is the hour for ablutions. And no water is holier than that of the Ganges. Men, women and children walk down the great stairways to the river and dip themselves in its Holy waters, which wash away all the pollutions and defilements.

The women throw garlands of flowers into the river so that it almost seems to be a flowing garden of flowers.

Fakirs, as immovable as marble columns, stand lost in mute contemplation, with one hand stretching out to the rising sun. From the heights of the terrace the Brahmins exhibit the holy lingers to the mass. On the other side of the river the architecture of the palaces draws itself to the blue skies. The temples rise with their pyramids of cut-stone where-on are portrayed the images of the gods and of the symbolic and sacred animals. Everywhere appears an extravagance of sculpture, a monstrous florescence of stone. Within the halls there cower enormous cattle made of marble. Then the almost infinitely repeated image of Ganesha, the god of wisdom, the god with the elephant's head.

The ablutions are completed; the music resounds from the temple the populace mass their way in. The marble columns with their images of the gods are decorated with flowers, but practically all of the gifts are brought to the lingam, which the women crown with velvet flowers moistened with dissolved butter.

Fakirs promenade about entirely naked, their bodies besmeared with cow-dung. Others haunch themselves down in the position of corpses as naked as the fomer and covered only with the traditional cow-dung.

Images of Siva are carried on palanquins all around the temple. Siva the word, and Siva the power. The god, in whose indeterminate form (male and female alike) carries in one hand a lingam, in the other a phallus of gold. The priests clad in white, awe-inspiring, bear aloft the phallic emblems, before which the people prostrate themselves.

In front, in the moist of the flute players, prance about the bayaderes, their arms bare, their knuckles surrounded with silver bracelets, their fingers and toes loaded down with rings, and an immense gold ring hanging down from the right side of the nose. They rhythmically sway their hips and silver bells, attached to the flanges of their dress, musically tinkle thruout the hall. In the temple a Brahman, with bare head, crosses his legs and cries out: I am Brahma, I am the All.'

To the soft rhythm of the flutes and tomtoms the bayaderes turn themselves about and wildly gyrate themselves into sacred dislocations. Meanwhile the Brahmins have had brought the sacred phalli, silvered and decorated with jewelry. The believers worshipfully kiss them and moisten them with holy water from the Ganges. The women in hysteric positions embrace the monstrous symbol, frenziedly kiss it, and crown it with flowers. The sacred cows with the golden horns move thru the mass. Thereupon the Brahman rises and cries: *'We have washed ourselves pure in the filth of sins: Make us fruitful and fortunate.'* And, touching his navel and genital organ, he adds: "There dwell the fire, the sun and the moon.

Now he related to the worshipful listeners, who have also smeared themselves with cow-dung, the wondrous story of Krishna, who at the age of fifteen years had seduced and laid low all the cowherdesses of the country: he praises the powers of Siva, who unceasingly creates and destroys as the symbol of Nature.

In this secret orgy the participants, gorged with treat and spiritous drinks, worship the Sakti in the form of a woman; she is completely naked and placed upon a kind of pedestal; an initiate completing the sacrifice by the sexual act. The ceremonies usually end with general cohabitation, each pair representing and becoming identical with Siva and his Sakti. The believers must fulfill these actions, their thoughts having arisen to divine planes and theoretically disconnected from the mere satisfaction of sensuality.

The precepts teaching these customs are full of devout moral theories, and are supposed to be fulfilled even by ascetics. And this is a good illustration of what religion does to mankind. It drags man down to what appears to be the very lowest level. It is believed that the people of India are more fully enslaved by religion than those of any other country at this time, and their status could hardly be lower.

The high position of the people in this country is due to the fact that they are less religious than the people of any other nation. And they will move higher as their religion fades longer.

Chapter No. 15 – Magic Mate

"And God said, It is not good that the ran should be alone. I will make a help-meet for him" (Genesis. 2:18). The Path to the Glorious Life is not generally known. The books, the schools and the universities do not teach it. The Bible says, *'Strait is the gate, and narrow is the way which leadeth unto (the Glorious) Life, and few there be that find it'* (Mat. 7:14).

The help Meet was not created for the purpose of propagation, but for the purpose of being a companion for man. For it was not good that man should be alone.

Here is what the Bible says on that point, to-wit: *"And the rib, which God had taken from man, made he a woman, and brought her unto the man. And the man said, This is now bone of my bones, and flesh of my flesh: she shall be called Woman, because she was taken out of Man. Therefore, shall a man leave his father and his mother, and shall cleave unto his wife: and they shall be one flesh"* (Gen. 22-24).

This woman was a help-meet for man. She was his Magic Mate. She was made because it was not good for the man to be alone. She was his loving companion.

When the Mind, under proper training, has evolved to that stage where it can realize that there is really a Divine Plane from which man has fallen, and to which he should, must and will return, the perception then will dawn in his Mind that much which seems as Sexualism is not lust for rental sensation and pleasure, nor an urge to propagate, but the craving of the Mind for its Divine Mate to complete the divided Unit.

Man's existence as a self-generative, self-sufficient Spiritual Being depends upon himself. This means the closing of what the Ancient Magi called the South Gate. That was the esoteric term for the obliteration of the Path to Sexual Propagation on the beastilic plane. For a correct concept of the secret of Sexualism, we consult the Arcane Magic of the Ancient Magi, in which the principles of Microcosmic Propagation are considered in a sacred, solemn manner.

From their scientific philosophy we learn that the regular relationship between man and woman, as in modern carriage, is the prevailing cause of much of the emotional misery, physical distress, and humanistic degeneration that fills the world with suffering.

In its cosmic aspect, Sexualism represents the universal bipolar force of the positive phase of Creation that appears in man, and the passive phase that appears in woman. In the Spiritual Realm the Creative Force is not divided. And there was a time in ancient days when the Creative Force was not divided in the case of man. The woman was not created to complete the Creative Force in ran, but to be a companion for him, because it was not good that he should be alone.

The division of the Creative Unit which now prevails in the physical realm, is the result of physical degeneration, as we expounded in our great course, titled Secret of Regeneration. That is the basic reason why the two halves of the divided Unit are incessantly seeking for the reunion of their divided forces.

It is the misconception of this urge of the divided Unit to reunite that underlies the process of fornication and propagation on the beastilic level.

Even the Apostle Paul did not appear to understand the secret nature of this problem. But he did know that fornication was wrong and said so. He shouted:

"Let not sin (fornication) reign in your mortal body, that ye would obey it in the lust thereof. ... For sin (fornication) shall not have dominion over you; for ye are not under the law (of sexual propagation) but under grace (Spiritual Generation)" (Rom. 6:12, 14, 1 John 3:9, 10).

Then Paul more definitely defined 'sin" by declaring:

"He that committeth fornication sinneth against his own body." (1 Cor. 5:1, 6:18).

Paul constantly and consistently taught his followers to rise above the plane of propagation on the beastilic level. But that part of his preachment has never been popular with the people nor with the clergy.

To consume the vital essence of the body in the function of sexual propagation weakens the brain, dulls the senses, and deteriorates the body. According to the Bible, Methuselah did not begat his first child until he was 187, and lived 969 years. Jahor begat his first child at 29 and died at the age of 143.

The nearest approach to a definite statement of the true condition of the Lord of the whole earth (Zech. 4:14) appears in the Apocrypha, being that part of the ancient scriptures rejected by the Mother Church because it presented too much of the Ageless Wisdom of the Ancient Magi. In that rejected part appeared this statement:

"The Kingdom of God (Divine Man) shall come (again) and human perfection be attained (again) when the (divided) forces of the halves (man and women) shall become centered again in one body, and the outside and inside, the male with the female, in one body and one flesh." (Gen. 2:24).

In the Life Cycle the ultimate destiny of Man is a return to the original state, the state of Androgyny.

In his original perfection, man was androgynous, and to that perfect state he will eventually return. This is vouchsafed in the Bible in these words: *"The thing that hath been, it is that which shall be (again)"* (Eccl. 1:9). According to the Ancient Magi, androgyny is a state that will return in the longer life cycles, of which one incarnation is but a day. Then there will be a reversion of the body's internal polarity, causing the creative essence to flow from the spinal base upward to the brain to increase man's consciousness, as symbolized by the two serpents

www.ingramcontent.com/pod-product-compliance
Lightning Source LLC
Chambersburg PA
CBHW050215270326
41914CB00003BA/428